George H Moss Jr

Karen L. Schnitzspahn

Victorian Summers

at the Grand Hotels
of Long Branch, New Jersey

George H. Moss Jr.

Karen L. Schnitzspahn

Foreword by John T. Cunningham

Ploughshare Press

Sea Bright, New Jersey

For the newest members of the sixth generation
of the Moss Family at the Jersey Shore

Catherine Elizabeth Silva

Hayley Elizabeth Moss
Bennett Davis Moss

━━━━━━━━━━

For

Nancy and Ginny

K.L.S.

Library of Congress Control Number: 00-092748
ISBN: 0-912396-09-1
Printed in the United States of America

Contents

Victorian Summers
at the Grand Hotels of Long Branch, New Jersey

Foreword

BY JOHN T. CUNNINGHAM

Very little on-site evidence remains of the Victorian days when Long Branch was the most elegant, most frequented and at times the most law ignoring resort on the Atlantic Coast. The grand wooden hotels have burned, fashions have changed and stringent laws have eliminated the old Monmouth Race Track and the gambling parlors. Interest shifted elsewhere – to Atlantic City before the 19th century ended and to more distant Miami and Las Vegas as the 20th century sped by.

Those of us vitally interested in New Jersey history in general and Jersey Shore history in particular know much of the Long Branch framework, enough to stir curiosity about what Long Branch and its denizens really looked like in the resorts' 19th-century heyday. We wish for authentic descriptions of what its visitors wore and ate, where they slept, where they played, and how they regarded the beach in an era of rigid morality regarding beach attire.

Who among us has not been stirred on first seeing Winslow Homer's elegant painting, "On the Bluff at Long Branch?" Painters can embellish what they see, of course, and Homer undoubtedly did so, but his vision of windblown young women atop the bluff is a lingering sensation. More realistic, more demanding and closer to reality are engravings and photographs. There, George H. Moss Jr. of Rumson has served us well for nearly 40 years.

Moss first brought the Monmouth County scene – and his remarkable collections of illustrative material – to the public in 1964 with his *NAUVOO TO THE HOOK*. Since then in five copiously-illustrated books he has given us five graphic photographic insights on the Monmouth coast (one of them with Karen Schnitzspahn, who is co-author of this book).

Anyone who goes beyond the American Revolution or the Civil War inevitably becomes charmed, and sometimes bewildered by the Victorian period. We lavish our attention on an architecture that features whimsical "carpenter Gothic" and its hand-sawn wooden decorations. Inevitably we are drawn to the lavish clothing, the heavy furniture, the large families, the heavy meals, the sentimental greeting cards and the striking gap between the very wealthy and the extremely poor.

Wealthy Victorians, like wealthy people in any time, needed a way to spend money in a fashion that would insure they were seen and admired. Long Branch after the Civil War fitted the need superbly. It was close to America's largest concentration of wealth in the suburbs of New York City and Philadelphia. Dependable trains linked those monied people with Long Branch, the first major stop on the tracks leading south along the shore. Eventually rails also connected Philadelphia and The Branch.

In *VICTORIAN SUMMERS*, George Moss and Karen Schnitzspahn follow the rich and the famous as they trekked toward what fit their desire for comfortable, even luxurious, lodgings and an insatiable need for activity to suit their high style and their quest for excitement.

Wherever Americans with money or celebrities (with or without money) went in the Victorian age, reporters and artists from the illustrated weeklies of the day – most notably *Harper's Weekly* and *Frank Leslie's Illustrated Newspaper* – followed.

When the crème de la crème traveled in those days they carried large trunks filled with the clothes they would need for a week or for the summer, as well as books, games, umbrellas, bathing gear, jewelry and whatever else they deemed vital to a summer of content. It is not a matter of conjecture, the artists were there to prove it for their magazines, newspapers (and not incidentally in this book, for generations to come).

If the drawings and sketches compiled by Moss and Schnitzspahn are to be believed, and there is no reason to doubt that, the ocean held only modest charms for women of the era. They are seen mostly sitting in the sand, carefully protecting their precious skins from the sun with umbrellas or occasionally, with heavy blankets.

Many members of the fashionable set did not really come to Long Branch for the bathing, any more than modern travelers frequent Atlantic City hotels for the salt water or ocean breezes. It was fashionable in the 1880s to stay in the hotel, enjoying the calorie-laden meals, the chance to rest on a luxurious bed and (for males only) the chance to put one's money where one's convictions lay in matters involving dice and playing cards.

Gambling was the rage, in well-appointed gambling rooms in the big hotels or at Monmouth Park (opened on July 30, 1870) for improvement of the breed and the thinning of spectator wallets. While reporters claimed women eschewed betting in the parlors, the ladies were free with their bets at the racing park. The fact that the betting at the track was controlled by the same men who ran the betting tables in the hotels did not seem to matter.

In September 1876, Olive Logan wrote in *Harper's New Monthly Magazine*, using as a theme the notion that "fashion is a queer moralist:"

> ...betting is freely and openly indulged in by many ladies as well as gentlemen who have been taught to look upon gambling as a terrible vice. Nor do they confine themselves to betting such trifles as loves and bon bons, but boldly to lose hundreds of dollars.

All of the famous, the infamous and occasionally the struggling, stayed at one of the so-called grand hotels on the bluff. That is the basic focus of *Victorian Summers*. The authors concentrate on ten "grand hotels," all of them huge, wooden structures subject to the pounding of the elements and the ever-present scourge of fire.

All those hotels would succumb to passing time, but that is only a moderate concern of George Moss and Karen Schnitzspahn. Their intent is to take us back to the glory days, to see the patrons, their luggage and their receptions in the hotels; to sit with them on the beach and to attend the races at Monmouth Park; to read the accounts as written by visiting journalists, a few of them critical but most them lavish in their praise of this empress of resorts.

It was, as a Charles Dickens character said, "a short life but a merry one." In its own unique fashion, *Victorian Summers* takes us on a closeup return to 125 years ago. We see it in the photography and the etchings, the playbills and the advertisements, the menus and the venues.

New Jersey and The Jersey Shore needed this intimate look at the gold coast of the fading Victorian Age. We never again will see it like it was. Even Atlantic City, for all its glitter and tinsel, makes little effort to hide the fact that it is only a center of gambling. The ocean is as far from Casino thoughts as if it were a thousand miles to the east. That was never so with Victorian Long Branch. It was alive, vibrant, varied and caring.

John T. Cunningham, author of 42 books on New Jersey, including a recently-published pictorial history of Atlantic City, has been called "Mr. New Jersey" by a variety of agencies, including Rutgers University when it awarded him one of the nine honorary degrees he holds. His reputation as New Jersey's best-known historian has been established for at least two decades. He is now at work on a short history of Ellis Island and the saga of immigrants.

Preface

When, through archaeology, a lost city or an ancient culture is unearthed, the past is often brought dramatically back to life. While archaeologists dig for artifacts, historians or "paper archaeologists" dig for facts. Their goal is the same – to discover the past and preserve it for the future.

My more than fifty-year interest in the history of the Jersey Shore – from Sandy Hook to Ocean Grove – has resulted in a specialized and ever-expanding collection of original observations, illustrations and ephemera spanning three centuries.

What is rewarding is that the written word found in the social commentaries of the day, plus the artistic wood engravings and photographic documentation of the Victorian era, vividly re-create, in exquisite detail, a singular and unique chapter of Monmouth County's past. Early newspapers have preserved the observations of their astute writers. Through the years, dozens of guidebooks have also preserved varied and detailed descriptions of the many attractions that brought fascinated first-time visitors to Long Branch.

HARPER'S WEEKLY and *FRANK LESLIE'S ILLUSTRATED NEWSPAPER* were two of the most popular of the early illustrated publications. They are a great source of extremely accurate and delightfully artistic scenes of life at the shore. Some of America's greatest artists (including Winslow Homer) produced magnificent illustrations of the Victorian period for those publications. Those were the days

before photographs could be reproduced in that particular media.

A few local photographers however, including Pach Brothers and Colwell Lane, actually did document this period. Some of their original efforts have survived in photography's most popular form of the day – the stereograph. Many of their images are the only known photographic examples of what life was truly like between 1859 and 1880 – the height of the Victorian period at Long Branch.

While grandeur and elegance best describe what has often been called the "Golden Age," it was also an age touched by pride and prejudice. That, however, is another story.

Situated on a bluff overlooking the Atlantic Ocean, Long Branch, New Jersey, was a well documented and an extremely popular internationally known "watering place" during the heyday of the Victorian era. Now, however, it is obvious that the dark covering clouds of time are fast obscuring its importance and the way it was a little more than a century ago.

VICTORIAN SUMMERS re-creates the way of life during that glorious period of time when the "grand hotels" of Long Branch were, indeed, "grand!" It is a broad but detailed picture of the daily routines, varied activities and special attractions at these hotels that introduced thousands of delighted visitors to this city by the sea. This book is not about the magnificent summer homes at the

Jersey Shore nor is it about the wealthy and well known families who found Long Branch a more than pleasant retreat. While certainly part of the history of this area, that, too, remains yet another story. This story is about a significant part of our history that is fast fading into obscurity. Its focus is specifically on Ocean Avenue's grand hotels and the activities of those summer visitors during the Victorian era.

Two attractions in the 1870s did much to vastly improve the hotel business and the local economy. The first was horse racing at nearby Monmouth Park in 1870. The second attraction was the great Ocean Pier that opened in 1879. Racing at Monmouth Park proved to be a popular event for decades. As a result, many race track enthusiasts became patrons of the Long Branch hotels. Located in front of LELAND'S HOTEL, the impressive Ocean Pier, at the height of its popularity, also played an important part in the daily social routine of many visitors. At the races, on the beach or on the boardwalk, Long Branch was the center of the social world.

For me, this volume fulfills a long desired goal — to preserve one of the most socially and historically significant periods of time at the Jersey Shore. Also, I have been motivated because my grandfather, Gernando Pannaci, was involved in the hotel business in Long Branch. In 1899 he purchased a hotel on Ocean Avenue formerly owned by Anthony Iauch. As a toddler in the 1920s, I remember visiting my grandmother, Annie, who continued to operate the hotel for another decade after her husband passed away. Memories are made of this.

The words and illustrations in this book are the observations and creations of gifted writers, artists and photographers of the period who pre-served those VICTORIAN SUMMERS AT THE GRAND HOTELS OF LONG BRANCH. All the illustrations in this book are from the Moss Archives unless otherwise credited.

Acknowledgements are in order for the invaluable contributions made by the following individuals who shared significant items from their own collections and gave permission to include them in this book: Thanks to Phil Delcamp for his STETSON HOUSE and OCEAN HOTEL ephemera; to Ken Rosen for his two interesting Long Branch stereographic views and to Jane C. Meehan for use of ephemera relating to KOLB'S HOTEL.

Mary Ann Kiernan of the Monmouth County Archives, deserves thanks for solving the seemingly unsolvable mysteries of certain of these grand hotels and bringing to light the otherwise missing pieces of their individual history.

I would especially like to thank my good friend Karen L. Schnitzspahn for working with me on this book. An author or coauthor of seven books, Karen's concentration on research and detail is well reflected in her writing. It is a pleasure to work with someone so dedicated to accuracy and preserving history. Our common interest in early photography as well as the Victorian era at the Jersey Shore resulted in working together to create THOSE INNOCENT YEARS, IMAGES FROM THE PACH PHOTOGRAPHIC COLLECTION 1898-1914.

Both Karen and I wish to take this opportunity to sincerely thank John T. Cunningham for his interest in our newest endeavor. We are very grateful and honored that he has written the foreword to VICTORIAN SUMMERS.

George H. Moss Jr.
September 2000

Why Look Back at the Victorian Era?

What is so enticing about the Victorian years and why are we still influenced by nineteenth century styles and customs today? Perhaps it has something to do with the incredible attention to details and the craftsmanship of that era. The intricacy of handmade tatting on a collar, the elegance of roses embossed on a silver spoon, and the softness of a plush velvet chaise represent the kinds of Victorian things that we admire.

Perhaps the way that Victorians took more time to do things and to do them well is of interest to us today as we look for faster modems for our computers and find it hard to exist without a cell phone. Maybe we idolize those lazy, unhurried days of people riding in horsedrawn carriages, swinging in hammocks, sipping tea from translucent china cups, and writing letters by hand on linen stationery. While waiting in traffic or trying to decipher food labels, we may wish for a return to a simpler time when most vegetables were organically grown and there was less traffic and fewer people! Conceivably, we look back to escape, to put ourselves into a world that we perceive as gentler and more virtuous.

There is no denying that there also existed a dark, down side to the Victorian era. Wars, disease, poverty, child labor, political corruption, murder, opium addiction, gambling, and prostitution - these evils and more pervaded the Victorian times. The era spanned the reign of England's Queen Victoria (1837 - 1901) and encompasses the wonders of the industial revolution with countless inventions. The people of the nineteenth century were no doubt concerned with speed and desired faster transportation and communication. It was a time of colonial expansion. There were great contrasts of excessive wealth and extreme poverty. And yet the connotation of "Victorian" that endures today is most often one of peaceful bliss and carefree days.

For over twenty years, I've been researching and writing about various aspects of life in the nineteenth and early twentieth centuries at the New Jersey Shore where I have resided for thirty years. My interest began in the early 1970s when I first read *Double Exposure* by George H. Moss Jr. I would often gaze at the nineteenth century photographs in that book as a way to relax. The antique stereo images of the local shore area literally popped out, and beckoned me to take a look at what it was like so long ago. The lure of the past captivated me and stimulated my ongoing interest in not only the early photography, but also the fashions and customs of the Victorian era at the shore.

Eventually, I met author and historian George H. Moss Jr., and he became my friend and mentor. In the early 1990s, I worked with George as coauthor of *Those Innocent Years, Images from the Pach Photographic Collection 1898-1914.* The creation of that book proved to be a marvelous experience. Now, with this book, I've been fortunate to have yet another opportunity to work with George and to go back even further in time than in our previous endeavor. I've learned more about the grand hotels and the nineteenth century pier that once existed by the oceanfront where I often walk the boards. I've enjoyed researching the vintage Victorian fashions and the origins of the Monmouth Park racetrack. It's been a fascinating journey, and I feel certain that readers will delight in the pleasures of *Victorian Summers.*

Karen L. Schnitzspahn
September 2000

"The Sea Side" — from drawings of OUR WATERING PLACES AT LONG BRANCH
by noted illustrator and political cartoonist, Thomas Nast.

HARPER'S WEEKLY, AUGUST 26, 1865

"View of Long Branch, thirty miles from New York City."
Frank Leslie's Illustrated Newspaper, Aug. 22, 1857

The Early Years

Agrowing seaside resort for almost a century, Long Branch, New Jersey, had attained an international reputation by 1870 as America's foremost "watering place." For decades it was known both as the "Brighton of America" and as the "American Boulogne." Situated on a natural bluff, the "Branch" delighted generations of visitors with an unparalleled view of the ever-changing Atlantic Ocean. Whether on calm waters or stormy seas, picturesque sailing vessels often added perspective to a breathtaking panorama.

In a way, nature was the great attraction. The refreshingly cool afternoon breeze that would sweep in over the ocean lured sweltering city dwellers from neighboring New York and Philadelphia to Monmouth County's "City by the Sea."

Apparently, the first Long Branch boarding house, previously a private residence, opened its doors to guests in 1788. A few years later, in May of 1792, a Philadelphia publication carried a notice of what, in reality, might be the first Long Branch hotel on the bluff. (The use of "House," "Boarding House" or "Hotel" often described the same type of establishment depending on size and services):

> "The subscribers beg to acquaint the public in general, and their friends in particular, that they continue in the same line of business in the house they occupied last year at the seashore in Shrewsbury, and have provided themselves with good waiters and laid in a good stock of liquors and everything necessary for the entertainment of ladies and gentlemen, and have provided large and commodious stables. They have also erected houses for the convenience of bathing, and will omit nothing to render the entertainment of those that may please to favor them with their custom in every respect agreeable. HERBERT and CHANDLER."[1]

In 1793, a Mr. Charles Biddle noted in his diary "lodged at CAPTAIN GREEN'S" (later the old BATH HOTEL):

> "The most agreeable place to spend some days in the summer that I know is Long Branch. There you have good living, a fine country to ride or walk in, a number of vessels constantly in sight, and generally good society."

Word was spreading and it was soon recognized that Long Branch was a special place for a summer vacation. In 1797 Jedidiah Morse in his book, *The American Gazetteer*, commented in particular about the summer visitors:

> "Much genteel company from Philadelphia and New-York resort here during the summer months for health and pleasure."[2]

A seventy-mile trip by stage from Philadelphia via Camden and Freehold to Long Branch in 1834 was often a tiring two-day adventure! In spite of that, many visitors thought it well worth the trip. However, an article offering some surprisingly negative comments about this resort was published in 1839 in the *Knickerbocker*, a New York monthly magazine. The well-travelled author, identified only as "L.C.N.," made some interesting personal observations. He wrote:

> "Of all places of summer resort, commend me to the Branch. I have spent years of summers at watering places; have walked the pump-rooms at Bath and Cheltenham; ...I have bathed and danced at Brighton; have played roulette and chatted French with the fair-haired, blue-eyed damsels at the Rhine...I have also wended my way up the noble Hudson in a magnificent steamer in company with a multitude of pilgrims of fashion to Saratoga; and yet I say, of all the watering places, give me Long Branch.
>
> The summer of 1838 we all remember to have been one of intense heat. Every watering place, far and near, was crowded to overflowing. The Branch had a benefit it had not known for years.
>
> The society last season, was as usual almost exclusively Philadelphians, and among them were some beautiful women, and some bred and born gentlemen, too, with whom it was a pleasure to associate; but in spite of good society, books, bathing, riding, etc., we could hardly prevent some very heavy hours accumulating upon our hands. Various were the endeavors made to get up amusements, of some kind; for be it known, there are none at the Branch. Cards are forbidden; no billiard tables; nothing but two nine-pin alleys...
>
> The Branch has fallen from its high estate. Time was, and in my memory, too, when the esplanade in front of Sears (Sairs) presented the gay scene of a tournament. Knights curvetted and charged, in ranks and squadrons, and right

forms of war. The long balconies were filled with bright eyes and fair forms..."

Continuing his article, the author refers to the past August of 1838. Apparently tournaments were still being held but, alas, were of "low" quality. His next statements are rather surprising!

> "For far and near it has been given out, that the young gentlemen of the different (boarding) houses would on this day divert their lady loves with a chasse au cochon, - a pig chase!
>
> This once delightful resort is going down hill. The ocean is making yearly inroads upon the bank...But be that as it may; the air and the water are the same, though ever changing; and in both, to the few who can rightly appreciate them, will be found society and health."[3]

In spite of the "pig chase" and the lack of entertainment, as time went by, Long Branch improved and soon earned many positive comments and soon regained its status of previous years. In 1841, for example, *Tanner's Central United States Guidebook* proclaimed it:

> "...A celebrated watering place, on the shore of the Atlantic Ocean, seventy-three miles from Philadelphia, and forty-five from New-York. There are, in addition to four extensive and commodious boarding-houses, several private establishments, where, with less parade and show of "style," the invalid may enjoy the refreshing sea air, and bathing, in their utmost perfection, and at a moderate expense - whilst those who inhabit the former are expected, and expect to pay liberally for their extravagant accommodations."[4]

Through the years dozens of different Long Branch boarding houses and hotels catered to generations of eager and enthusiastic, as well as impatient and demanding, summer visitors.

A few of the older hotels were originally farm houses. They became boarding houses and, in turn, were often remodeled and enlarged into some of the popular establishments of the period. Newer and larger hotels soon followed and Long Branch eventually blossomed into America's premier summer resort.

In 1851 there appears to be seven "boarding houses" on the bluff. Some of the early hotels, still called "boarding houses," were much larger and hardly anything like the small boarding houses/farm houses found at the Branch in the late 1700's.

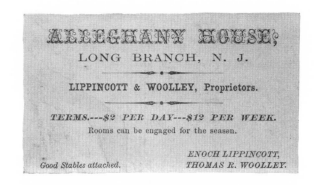

These are typical advertising cards of the smaller boarding houses and hotels in Long Branch (ca. 1855).

Most of these relatively new hotels overlooked the Atlantic Ocean and were either two or three stories high with piazzas or verandas running the entire length of the building at each level. J. W. MORRIS'S BOARDING HOUSE, for example, which opened for business on July 4, 1846, contained about thirty-five rooms in a modest two-story structure.

The growing popularity of Long Branch was well known. In September of 1853, William R. Morris wrote a letter back home from Angels Camp, California, to "Miss Mary E. Borden, Red Bank, Monmouth County, New Jersey." Morris had left Monmouth County a year earlier to seek his fortune in the gold mines of California. Among the many comments in his letter, one sentence is of particular interest: "I have heard that Long Branch is well supplied this summer with visitors – it is becoming a noted watering place."[5] Indeed it was!

In June of 1860, the Raritan and Delaware Bay Rail Road route from Port Monmouth to Red Bank extended its line to Eatontown and Long Branch. This made a direct contact between New York and the Branch. It was an eighteen-mile trip from New York to Port Monmouth by steamboat and then a

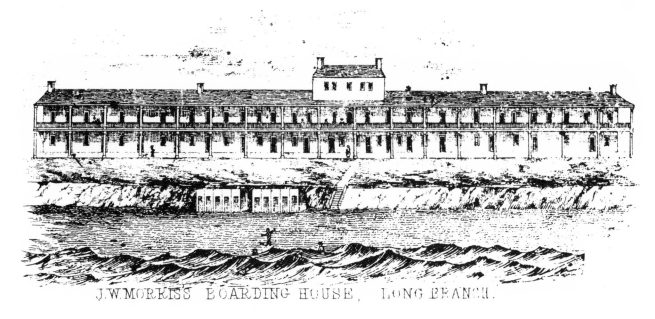

The MORRIS BOARDING HOUSE (later sold, enlarged and renamed the MANSION HOUSE) in one of the earliest known illustrations of a building on the bluff at Long Branch.

FROM J.B. SHIELDS MAP OF MONMOUTH COUNTY (LIGHTFOOT MAP) 1851

3

fifteen-mile railroad ride via Eatontown to Long Branch — a total time of two and a half hours.

The steamers *Rip Van Winkle* and *Alice Price* were chartered to convey distinguished guests (including both the New York and New Jersey Govenors) via this new Long Branch route for participation in the opening ceremonies.

> "The sail down the Bay, the ride of fifteen miles to Long Branch, a dinner, a sea-shore ramble, and the parade and review of the honored and splendidly-disciplined City Guards, combine to make the opening of the Railroad as pleasant an occasion as one often has the opportunity of enjoying."[6]

This was the beginning of the end of the glory days for many Shrewsbury River steamboats. Only a few survived this competition of a direct commute from New York to Long Branch. This innovative and appealing new route was actually a time saver.

> "By this road business people can leave the city at 4 o'clock P.M., take a sea bath at Long Branch at 7 o'clock, enjoy a good night's sleep, far removed from the terrible heat of the Metropolis, and return sure and certain at 6 in the morning; arriving in New York at half past eight. Citizens can thus be enabled to board their families at Long Branch all through the hot weather, they personally going to and returning from their business morning and evening.
>
> Besides an endless number of small hotels and boarding houses; in fact the farmers all over country take boarders, and taken altogether, not less than 8,000 visitors are accommodated at Long Branch every season. Now the Railroad is completed, the number will be increased immensely, and I already hear of a new hotel, capable of accommodating 1,000 visitors, in contemplation.
>
> Long Branch will become one of the most celebrated watering places on the continent. Its beautiful situation, the green country around, the great ocean in front, the mighty commerce of the world sweeping along by sail and steam, its easy access to New York and Philadelphia, its far famed sea bathing, and natural and artificial beauties and advantages combine to make it the most famous summer resort in the world."[7]

So stated a far sighted reporter for the *Monmouth Democrat* in July of 1860. By that time there were eleven very busy hotels established along Ocean Avenue.

Newspapers of the period captured much of the details of life at the shore, although sometimes accurate reporting was often overshadowed by the personal views of the unnamed writers. In an 1865 *New York Times* article entitled "Our Watering Places - Long Branch," a reporter wrote these interesting comments after a day's observation at this popular resort:

> "The hotels are fourteen in number. (Not all on Ocean Avenue.) Of these, about a dozen are called "first-class." I should not call them so, using my own judgement; but I suppose it is the price that regulates it, though in that case the whole fourteen are first- class," for they all charge $ 4 a day, or $ 21 per week. There are some farmhouses and cottages, I understand, where the board per week is as low as $ 18. The really first-class hotels are the MANSION HOUSE, the METROPOLITAN, CONGRESS HALL, the UNITED STATES, the PAVILION, the BATH, HOWLAND'S and the LAWN and this ought to be enough, in all conscience, but it isn't. These are almost always overcrowded. The hotels, I conclude from personal observation, are the two first named. They are the largest, the most elegant, and have the choicest representation of fashion, beauty, wealth and refinement. (You see I put refinement last; it is usually in a woeful minority at all Summer resorts.)"[8]

By 1868 there were just ten significant well-established hotels along the scenic bluff. These attractive hotels, with their large well-kept front lawns, afforded a sweeping view of both busy Ocean Drive (later Ocean Avenue) as well as the impressive sea. For almost three miles, this "Golden Promenade" provided visitors an opportunity to enjoy a short carriage ride (and be seen and admired) or to begin a daring and adventuresome drive into the countryside.

For almost the next fifty years the number of hotels on the bluff varied little at any given time. Older establishments either were renovated, enlarged or just changed names. Others burned or were torn down and often replaced by new hotels.

In Victorian times, for those who could afford a trip for a day, a week or even the entire season, surviving the oppressive health- threatening summer heat and disease-laden filth of the city meant an unforgettable summer at either the mountains or the seashore.

Newly arrived visitors to the seashore, for their comfort and delight, found splendid accommodations in some of the finest Victorian summer hotels of the period. Located on the now famous Long Branch Bluff, these grand hotels captured the cooling effect of the ocean breeze and provided a welcome oasis during the insufferable heat of the summer season.

These impressive establishments catered to a variety of pocketbooks. In the finest hotels, the most ostentatious and demanding patron found his every request filled in minutes. Those of more modest means found pleasure in less imposing surroundings.

Another journalistic opinion describing "Long Branch, The American Boulogne" appeared in late August of 1871 in a weekly publication called *EVERY SATURDAY*. It reads in part:

"All the chief hotels, as we have said, face the beach, looking toward it from the westerly side of Ocean Avenue. They are mostly long narrow buildings of wood, rather cheap and flimsy looking as a rule, with pillar-supported balconies flush with every story but the highest, and extending the entire length of the structure; a broad piazza below, in view of the sea, and exposed to its cooling wind, attracts promenaders. In front and separating the house from the street lies a smooth green lawn sacred to croquet and childish sports. The avenue itself is situated almost upon the verge of the bluff, divided from it only by an interjacent strip of grass from fifty to a hundred feet wide, or even narrower than that. Starting from the front of any one of these great houses, one crosses the road, and following a gravelled path finds himself in half a minute in full view of the beach, and at the head of a flight of steps, around the foot of which upon the sand cluster in ragged rows the rough little bathing-houses which pertain to the hotel. To right and left, dotted along the bluff, wherever similar stairs

Entitled "Long Branch,' this sketch illustrates some of the attractions that brought so many visitors to the Branch. The surf, beach, bath houses and the bluff are prime examples. People also liked to stroll along the bluff socializing and observing the stylish carriages on busy Ocean Avenue and the grand hotels in the background.
THE NEW JERSEY COAST AND PINES BY GUSTAV KOBBÉ

descend are little wooden structures open upon the sides, but roofed, and furnished with comfortable rows of seats."[9]

FRANK LESLIE'S ILLUSTRATED NEWSPAPER, during the summer season of 1872, offered a further description of the "City by the Sea" –

"– the Branch is recognized as the American Brighton – the summer home of wealth, rank and beauty. Each year adds to its popularity. Channels of pleasure open on every side. Ocean Avenue - broad, long and smooth (the finest drive in the world) is a delight in itself...

One can scarcely understand the nature of the spot. At one moment the visitor is looking off the bluff far out on the seemingly quiet water, or plunging through the glorious surf; a few moments later he roams in the garden district of the State, surrounded with luxuriant foliage and choice fruit...

The lawn in front of the hotels filled with merry children, the little summer-houses on the bluff with older persons of tender thoughts. The beach dotted with promenaders venturing boldly toward the water, then dodging hastily back to escape the mounting surf, the waves themselves playing all sorts of antics with the bathers - these glimpses tell us that the season is opened in very truth!"[10]

Another significant article reflecting the continued interest in this popular sea-side resort was written for *HARPER'S WEEKLY* in the following summer of 1873:

"Long Branch, a post village and watering place of Monmouth County, New Jersey, on the sea-coast about thirty-three miles south of New York. Here are several boarding-houses and good bathing-grounds, which are much frequented by the citizens of New York and Philadelphia."

Such was the Long Branch of only a few years ago, as described in *LIPPINCOTT'S GAZETTER*. It was then a quiet, retired spot where a few families used to resort to enjoy the advantages of seclusion, sea-air and surf bathing. In less than ten years its character has entirely changed. For upward of nine miles along the bluff which overlooks the ocean beautiful cottages rise at intervals, surrounded by pleasant grounds on which the landscape gardener has expended all the resources of his art; magnificent hotels offer accommodations for thousands of guests; and along the sandy strip of

These two young ladies enjoying "A Drive to Elberon," perhaps to visit a friend, were sketched by artist C. S. Reinhart. The parade of horses and carriages on Ocean Avenue was a delight to see. The fashions and equipages of the day were often a subject of much conversation at social gatherings.
HARPER'S NEW MONTHLY MAGAZINE, SEPTEMBER 1886

beach at the foot of the bluff innumerable bathing-houses have been erected.

Already it is the favorite and most fashionable watering-place in the United States, having outstripped Newport, with its two hundred years of celebrity, and Saratoga, with its century's start in advance, and there seems to be no obstacle to its indefinite growth in the future. The extension of the New Jersey Central Railroad to Long Branch, which there is little reason to doubt will be completed the ensuing fall, will add largely to the prosperity and popularity of the place." [11]

Seemingly always in print, each new description of Long Branch, however, offered more insight into its past. This example was published in an 1875 guidebook entitled *POPULAR RESORTS AND HOW TO REACH THEM*.

"Long Branch, one of the most popular seaside resorts in America, is in Monmouth County, N.J. It was visited for health and recreation previous to 1812; and soon after the termination of the war with Great Britain, hotels were opened for the accommodations of visitors.

Still its magnitude is of recent growth; and the last fifteen years have done more for its development and improvement than the preceding fifty had accomplished. Its hotel accommodations are sufficient for fifteen thousand persons; yet each recurring season crowds them to their full capacity. Elegant and spacious cottages, owned and occupied by persons of distinction, line the principal avenues for long distances...

The beach at Long Branch is famous for its natural grandeur, as well as for its artificial attractions. It is an open bluff, rising some twenty feet or more above the tide-line, and extending a distance of five miles. Along this, the grand drive is constructed, and the principal hotels are erected. Here, doing the season, showy and elegant equipages dash, in passing and repassing lines, while the verandas and porticoes are thronged with spectators. No view could be more animated or attractive than this, with its life, gayety, and beauty, relieved by the wide and restless ocean, swelling and rolling in boundless perspective." [12]

During most of the Victorian years, Long Branch enjoyed a fine ongoing reputation. Written observations can be found in many original newspapers, magazines and popular guidebooks of the past. Fortunately, the articles in those publications have provided excellent documentation of the changing times. It is also interesting that these observations vary depending on the interpretation of the different writers through the years. An article in 1879 provides a new look at the Branch:

"Long Branch, N.J., has become famous as the resort of the more wealthy and fashionable classes of New York and Philadelphia, and in the minds of the majority of those who have never visited it, there is probably an impression that it is unsuited to people of moderate means and quiet tastes. This is, however, a great misconception. The charges at the hotels range from three dollars to four dollars per day, and from twelve dollars per week, upwards. The carriage fares are also very moderate, and need exclude none who do not own their own teams – and those constitute three-fourths – the pleasure of the drive. There is less attempt at vain display and less excitement than at many less noted and cheaper resorts. Fashion decrees no particular course of conduct or style of dress, and there is enough democratic leaven in the lump to make it proper for every one to do as he pleases, provided the ordinary proprieties of life are observed. It is a place to come to for rest, and in the contemplation of the grand in nature, and the attractive in art, it will be a rest most beneficial to both body and mind." [13]

Once again, almost a decade later, at the end of the 1883 summer season, a detailed account appeared of the most recent status of the Branch at that time.

"So many causes have operated to bring the name of Long Branch before the public that its reputation is, perhaps, even more wide-spread than that of Saratoga. During President Grant's administration it was virtually the summer capital of the country, and a view of its sun-lit sea brought comfort to the death-bed of President Garfield. It has been the scene of important cabinet meetings, and of protracted sessions of Congressional committees. In the palmy days of Fisk, Tweed, and their followers, Long Branch became notorious for its profligacy, and for the lavish expenditure of money and ostentatious display of wealth by those mushroom millionaires.

At that time its reputation was so unsavory, that many pious persons termed it the "Devil's Stronghold." To this day, the rural visitor to

New York whose curiosity impels him to run down to "the Branch" does so with feelings similar to those with which he first steps inside a theatre.

The Long Branch of to-day is, however, a far different place from that of twelve or fifteen years ago. Then it was an isolated cluster of hotels, bounded on either side for miles by stretches of lonesome beach, of which the solitudes were unbroken by human habitations. Now it forms but a small part of the great cottage city that extends, with almost unbroken ranks, from Sandy Hook to Barnegat, and which during the summer months transforms the once desolate wastes of yellow sand into scenes of abounding life and ceaseless activity.

...What the houses lack in color is partly compensated in design, and by the surroundings of those situated a short distance back from the coast, where the landscape gardener has found opportunities for the exercise of his art. The country between Long Branch and the Shrewsbury River, including Rumson's Neck, is a revelation of what may be accomplished in the way of landscape by the combination of nature and art supported by wealth. Its roads are hard, smooth and well shaded, and for miles the adjourning grounds, in the midst of which are set architectural gems of chalet-like cottages or more pretentious dwellings...

Long Branch, being the oldest of the coast settlements, retains many hotel buildings which, while comfortable and well located, are relics of the time when every carpenter was his own architect, and houses were built and added to in compliance with the exigencies of their occupants, rather than with a view to external appearance. In contrast to the severe simplicity of these reminders of the past are the gaudy structures which, under the name "clubhouse," have recently been erected by gamblers for business purposes, and in which their trade is carried on day and night with an ever-increasing run of custom.

That peculiar imitation of young manhood, recently classified as the "dude" seems to find Long Branch a congenial haunt, and there attains the perfection of his species. The sensation of this summer's season at the WEST END hotel has been the appearance of the "Prince of Dudes," a being whose sole apparent object of existence is the display and the rapid change from one to another of various costumes of gorgeous raiment. His ambition in life seems to be that of impressing the spectator

with his utter helplessness and inability to perform, unaided, any act demanding physical or mental exertion. Long Branch is, however, so easily accessible from New York that a large number of business men of the city find it convenient to run down every evening to their summer homes on its breezy coast, and this the young women of its hotels and cottages are not entirely dependent upon the feeble-minded dudes for masculine society or for partners at the hotel hop."[14]

While the many descriptions of the hotels, the bluff and Ocean Avenue might appear somewhat repetitious, each, in its own way, is another valuable glimpse into the past. All of these comments provide added insight into life during those Victorian days at Long Branch.

What a difference each year made in appearance and the way of life at the shore. Gustav Kobbé, a well-known critic and writer is probably best remembered for his illustrated and popular book, THE NEW JERSEY COAST AND PINES, published in 1889. Kobbé made some interesting comments in this book. His keen observations of the latest changes taking place at the Branch are well expressed.

"The Long Branch of today is a sea-shore cosmopolis. The features which attract the vast summer throng to it probably repel as many...it is "fashionable" in the sense in which the word is used by those who fondly imagine that lavish display of wealth is evidence of high social position. In fact the display of wealth, whether in the equipages on Ocean Avenue, in the fabrics and jewels of evening toilets, at the gaming-table or on the race-track, seems to be the chief amusement of a large majority of successors of the worthy Philadelphians who over a century ago discovered the resort.

It may be judged from the foregoing that Long Branch is not a place whither a circumspect parent would take his family for a quiet summer by the sea; but for those who like to be in the whirl of a fashionable watering-place it is without a rival, as it is also for the cynic who enjoys drawing his own conclusions in regards to the maddening crowd as it moves aimlessly by. Ocean Avenue in itself is a beautiful thoroughfare, a broad drive-way along the five miles of bluff, commanding a superb view of the ocean and swept by its cooling breezes...towards evening, (it) is probably the liveliest thoroughfare in the United States. Here

"The Drive." This illustration by renowned artist Granville Perkins captures a lively late afternoon on Ocean Avenue more than a decade before Gustav Kobbe's own written description of a similar scene.

APPLETON'S JOURNAL, SEPTEMBER 7, 1872

one can see almost every kind of vehicle - stages crowded with excursionists, buggies drawn by swift roadsters, tandems, four-in-hands, T-carts etc...

....many of them perfectly appointed and each interesting in its own way, as representing one of the many types of people to be found at this resort. Among the turnouts are many from the resorts north and south of Long Branch, whose residents doubtless look with quiet amusement upon much of what they see.

Even to those who would not care to live there, Long Branch is interesting if only as an object-lesson in certain extreme phases of American life - phases which could manifest themselves only in a country whose society is still undergoing the process of fermentation."[15]

And now, as we have recently entered a new millennium, Gustav Kobbé would yet be correct in saying "society is still undergoing the process of fermentation."

"On the Bluff at Long Branch, at the Bathing Hour" by Winslow Homer.
In this widely-recognized sketch of the Bluff, some well-dressed women cope with the ocean breeze as they head down to the bath houses. One of America's foremost artists, Homer visited the Branch between 1869 and 1874 where he produced over a half dozen illustrations of the area. His well-known oil painting, "Long Branch, New Jersey," (1869) is another scene on the Bluff and belongs to the Museum of Fine Arts, Boston.

HARPER'S WEEKLY, AUGUST 6, 1870

This busy scene in the Ocean Hotel lobby shows the arrival of new guests as porters carry their heavy luggage upstairs to their rooms.

FRANK LESLIE'S ILLUSTRATED NEWSPAPER, JULY 6, 1872

The Fashionable Life

Packing for a trip to a Long Branch grand hotel during the Victorian era required time and patience. Servants would haul cumbersome wooden trunks and sturdy leather valises out from storage in posh city townhouses. Then, they would carefully fill them with the proper garments needed for their employer's seaside vacation.

To be proper, the Victorian seaside hotel guests' agenda required several changes of clothing each day for various activities. The act of getting dressed and groomed known as the lady's "toilette" represented a time-consuming activity. Today, people pack many outfits for a vacation at a resort hotel or on a cruise ship. But even at the grandest hotels or on the most luxurious ships, skimpy swim suits, shorts, and T-shirts are acceptable for daytime wear. Victorians, of course, did not possess such casual clothes that could easily be tossed into a suitcase. Their daytime apparel was far more complex and of course, far less re-

vealing! Manners and morals had to be strictly observed.

The ladies' clothing no doubt took up a great deal of space in the luggage. The billowing skirts of the early Victorian dresses required elaborate hooped petticoats and cage crinolines. By the 1870s, full skirts were replaced by styles with straighter fronts but sporting puffy bustles that needed elaborate structures inside them to exaggerate and supposedly enhance their backsides. It's always puzzling today to think of how Victorian women could ever sit while wearing a hoop or a bustle! Corsets made with whalebone stays to nip in the waist were also an essential part of a lady's daily wardrobe.

The dresses consisted of many yards of fine cotton, silk, or taffeta and required careful folding. Cleaning and pressing the garments represented a difficult task in those days before automatic washing machines and electric irons. Dur-

An 1885 advertisement from DEMAREST'S MAGAZINE describes the "Langtry" Bustle, named for English actress Lillie Langtry who frequented Long Branch. This form to enhance the backside featured springs that supposedly allowed the wearer to sit down comfortably. It is doubtful that the "Jersey Lily" endorsed the many products that used her name.

"During the Victorian era, summer vacationers most likely packed some contraptions such as this "Supporter and Skeleton Waist for hot weather."
HARPER'S WEEKLY, AUGUST 16, 1873

ing the hot, humid summers at the New Jersey shore, many changes of garments were needed for cleanliness alone.

The restrictions of movement evident in the fashions reflected the women's place in Victorian society. In the male-dominated nineteenth century, gentlemen could wear more comfortable clothes that were unacceptable for the ladies. American reformer Amelia Jenks Bloomer revolutionized women's clothing in the early 1850s with the introduction of her namesake, bloomers, or baggy pantaloons for active women. However, in general, apparel for ladies, even for sport, remained unwieldy and uncomfortable throughout the nineteenth century.

The excessive fashions signified the wealth of elite Victorians who could afford extravagant sojourns and their ever-growing participation in leisure time activities. Nevertheless, copies of the latest modes worn by the rich and famous became available to the public by the mid nineteenth century. By the mid-1860s, sewing machines became more widely used, and the introduction of the Butterick's graded paper pattern gave every woman the opportunity to make fashionable garments. But even if they wore similar styles, the working people still did not have the free time that the wealthier classes had nor could they afford to buy expensive fabrics and accessories or stay at grand hotels or lavish cottages for the summer. Often, domestics and children's nannies would accompany the family but, of course, their own wardrobes were far less elaborate.

A tasteful walking suit or dress was suitable for breakfast and a morning stroll on the boardwalk or beach. An 1877 article described breakfast time at a Long Branch hotel:

"At half-past eight the morning papers appear, the dailies monopolized and sold at six cents. By this time pedestrians, in ones and twos, are strolling on the bluff. At the breakfast table everybody is in lawn or linen, and the military-looking head-waiter only requires a cocked hat and staff to make a court chamberlin or drum major or parish beadle out of him. Ha! we have spring chicken, that bird of paradise, for breakfast. How strange, methinks, that chickens should be so perfect when eggs are so doubtful…"[1]

"Visitors sunning themselves after a bath."
FRANK LESLIE'S ILLUSTRATED NEWSPAPER, AUGUST 27, 1879

Another dress was required for lunch, a bathing costume for a dip in the surf, then perhaps an afternoon dress or outfit suitable for a carriage ride. For the evening, a lady would wear a fashionable dinner dress, and finally an elaborate fancy gown for those evenings when grand balls and hops took place. Other changes of clothing might be required for bowling, playing croquet, or going to the racetrack. It is fascinating to observe how ladies at the beach in their elegant dresses are often depicted sitting directly on the sand. It must have been quite an ordeal to shake all that sand out of the yards of fabric!

The vacationing women enjoyed showing off their fine jewelry. Dangling earrings, necklaces, bracelets, brooches, and rings can be observed in illustrations. Many frivolous-looking accessories were, however, really necessities for the Victorian lady. She would never venture out without a hat and a parasol to not only enhance a stylish outfit but also to protect her delicate skin from the sun. Parasols of embroidered silk and other fine fabrics are not to be confused with umbrellas for the rain. Close-fitting bonnets that tied under the chin

are seen in the early Victorian period with hat styles becoming larger and elaborately decorated with feathers and flowers as the nineteenth century progressed. Gloves added a chic accent and protected the hands from soil and sun. Fans that were used both for decoration and to keep cool came in many styles from the simplest palm leaf-shaped rattan ones for the beach to ornate folding silk fans for the fancy dress ball.

The Victorian fashions were not in sepia tones of brown or in black and white. Because that is what we see in vintage photographs and engravings, we sometimes forget that the colors worn in the nineteenth century once appeared vibrant and bright. Hues of sapphire blue, rusty garnet, lilac, and olive green are but a few examples of colors described in the fashion magazines of the era. Stripes and bold patterns were often favored. The Victorian custom of wearing black mourning clothes for prolonged periods of grieving may explain some of the heavy dark costumes that are also seen in illustrations of the era. Otherwise, the Victorians loved bright shades for their summer attire.

The hand coloring of fashions such as those in the popular *GODEY'S LADY'S BOOK* gives us an idea of the wide array of bright colors that were stylish. The ladies kept up with the latest modes in several weekly magazines. *HARPER'S BAZAR*, a popular publication, was mainly devoted to women's fashions and included instructions for embroidery and other embellishments.

Vacation wardrobes for the men were far simpler than the women's. The well-to-do men also wore fine fabrics but of course without all those yards of excess cloth. Nevertheless, a gentleman needed several changes of three-piece suits, a top hat, gloves, fine accessories, suspenders and garters, and of course a bathing suit with a top. (Tops were required for men's bathing suits at the Jersey Shore until the early 1940s!)

Children's clothes often mimicked the adult styles except that the dresses were a little shorter and usually worn with pantaloons under them. Little boys wore dresses even up to the age of five, and it is often hard to tell the sex of a young child in an illustration. For bathing, children appear comfortable playing in the sand in simple cotton or wool outfits with sailor suits and middy blouses being popular styles. This nautical look in bathing attire would become common for adult bathing costumes as well and remained popular through the early twentieth century.

Bathing represents the activity that seems to stir the most interest and often typifies the Victorian seashore. In those days, however, the main attraction was not swimming, but just being near the ocean to sniff the salt air and look at the view probably had as much or more importance. The fashionable hotel crowd delighted in showing off their finery and the main idea was to be seen as appearances were important.

A brief history of bathing costumes and customs provides a better look at the habits of Victorian beachgoers. The first bathhouse was said to open at the famous seaside resort of Brighton, England, in 1754. The ladies' bathing costumes consisted of ankle-length flannel robes that were tied at the neck. These suits supposedly billowed up around them in the surf creating a comical appearance. Nevertheless, this style continued until around 1850 when they were modified to include tighter fitting tops and ankle length pantaloons covered by a full skirt. Long Branch was even called "The American Brighton" and of course the bathing fashions from England were copied.

At first, bathing was considered not merely a leisure time activity, but a "prescription" even recommended by doctors for many ailments. The salt water was often called a healthful "tonic" that could invigorate both mind and body. A quick dip in the ocean was thought to be more beneficial than a longer swim. Most illustrations depict the salt water as cold and, no wonder, as the heavy restrictive bathing costumes must have made it seem even worse when they got saturated. Wool and serge became popular for bathing suits with the intention that they would keep warmth in when they were probably doing the complete opposite when wet!

Bathhouses on the beach that were set back by the Bluff are visible in many illustrations of Long Branch. The vacationers would change in a bathhouse to go for their dip, never in their hotel room. A delightful Long Branch stereo view by G.W. Pach, shows a bathhouse with an ad for *FRANK LESLIE'S LADY'S JOURNAL* painted in bold letters on the roof. In the photograph, we can see ladies on the beach in dresses with parasols, people bathing in the surf while holding the ropes, and bathing attire hanging out to dry on makeshift clothes poles in front of the bathhouses.

Characteristic of the firm Victorian morality, men and women followed many rules including separate bathing times. In the early days mixed bathing was prohibited. A flag would be raised to indicate which sex could go in the surf with a white flag as the signal for women, although their husbands were allowed to accompany them. A red flag was raised for the men's bathing time. However, this practice was eventually abandoned.

An 1878 publication lists the rules to follow for bathing. The writer's comments and list seem quite outdated and humorous today, and yet some information continues to hold true.

> "SEA BATHING. - It cannot be too forcibly impressed upon the visitor at the seashore that this preeminent feature of our watering place is a ready means for good or harm, according to the manner in which it is used. Those who emerge from the luxury of a bath and soon suffer the enervating effect of reaction, often conclude that sea-bathing 'does not agree with them,' and envy the apparently peculiar organization of others, who become vastly strengthened and built up in a regular systematic use of the same remedial agent. In nearly every

"Bathing Scene" at Long Branch.

PACH STEREOGRAPH #22, CA. 1870

"Ladies hiring bathing-suits."
Frank Leslie's Illustrated Newspaper,
August 23, 1879

*"Bathers receiving their valuables
from the deposit safe."*
Frank Leslie's Illustrated Newspaper,
August 23, 1879

such instance the fault lies with the individual, not in the bath. A few suggestions are condensed from a former work by the author, premising that the effects are stimulating or depressing, according to the degree of care exercised.

1st. Provide a proper suit of mohair (preferable) or flannel, made full - the lady's short skirt belted to the waist, shoes if necessary, though they are liable to fill with sand. Oil silk caps and broad-rimmed hats are used by the ladies.

2d. Select the time.— The white flag should indicate a rising tide, other hours are dangerous.

3d. Bathe before eating, and never on a full stomach, or within three hours after a meal.

4th. Ladies do not bathe before 6 o'clock A.M., as gentlemen are then especially privileged.

5th. The Five Minute Rule. - Physicians agree that beyond this limit an injurious reaction destroys the benefit obtained.

6th. Coming Out. - Dry off quickly and use friction and exercise; dress and walk rapidly;

avoid spirits. If convenient, dress lightly in your room for the bathing house.

7th Respect Timidity - Do not force the delicate into the water. Let them lie prone on the beach and meet the surf gently half way, till they embrace.

8th. Regard the Bathing Master. - He is supposed to know his business, and his directions should insure your safety. Nearly every bathing 'accident' has occurred in contravention of established rules."

The Victorian writer of rules for bathing concludes with some thoughts about health:

"The effect of the atmosphere and sea bathing is especially beneficial in cases of a paralytic or nervous character, rheumatism, kidney trouble and dyspepsia, etc.

The hot and cold sea water baths at the West-end Hotel and Borden's establishment at the lower end of the beach, are found exceedingly useful for invalids and others who would avoid the excitement of the surf."[2]

Written guidelines such as the ones quoted above are the observations of their author and are not necessarily all fact, but still furnish us with a

16

"On the beach of Long Branch from sketches by Fred E. Foster."

Harper's Weekly, August 4, 1877

"*American Sketches: Bathing at Long Branch.*"

THE ILLUSTRATED LONDON NEWS, SEPTEMBER 4, 1875

good overall idea of the customs as the words are coming directly from the era.

Illustrations as engravings by artists who visited the sites, or photographs, mostly stereo-views, of the Victorian seaside at Long Branch give an idea of the cavalcade of styles that could be observed. An 1875 sketch from the *ILLUSTRATED LONDON NEWS* provides a delightful artist's representation of beach life at Long Branch. Here, a variety of visitors can be seen in attire ranging from elegant afternoon dresses, hats, and parasols to the simple dresses and bathing costumes.

The article that accompanied this engraving describes Long Branch as "the immediate refuge of heat-exhausted New Yorkers," and "the most celebrated of all the surf-bathing resorts of America." The writer goes on to say, "People from all parts of the United States crowd to this place for a few days, a week, or longer, during the season, which extends from the 1st of July to the 1st of September. There is constant communication between Long Branch and New York, about twenty miles distant; and many citizens of the metropolis go down every evening after business hours, leaving their families there permanently. The 'Summer New York' as it is sometimes called, is given up to social gaieties, which extend to ab-solute dissipation. All fashionable distractions are as numerous and constant here in summer as during the height of mid-winter society life in the city."[3]

The competition among the well-to-do vacationers to be in style was obviously an integral part of Victorian hotel life at Long Branch. Everyone who was anyone summered at Long Branch in the mid-nineteenth century and an actors' colony thrived there. In those pre-movie days, great stage stars from New York and Philadelphia flocked to the Branch where they stayed at grand hotels. Some of them, such as Maggie Mitchell and Lester Wallack, purchased or rented cottages in the Elberon section. Just as people enjoy seeing what their favorite stars are wearing today, the vactioners at Long Branch eagerly vied to get a glimpse of what their stage idols were wearing.

The parade of finery - from the moment of arrival at the pier or railroad station, to strolls on the boardwalk and carriage rides on Ocean Avenue, from bathing hours to the formal balls and hops at the hotels - is well documented in the illustrations, photographs, and writings from the Victorian period. These depictions keep the colorful details of the era's fashions and customs alive for our study and enjoyment.

By the Sad Sea Waves.

19

A wood engraving of "The Race At Monmouth Park – On The Homestretch."
This scene, observed from The Club House, also captures some of the fashions of the day.
FRANK LESLIE'S POPULAR MONTHLY, JULY 1877

"The Principal Entrance To The Monmouth Park Race Course. From a photograph by A. J Russel."
FRANK LESLIE'S ILLUSTRATED NEWSPAPER, JULY 13, 1872

Monmouth Park

On July 30, 1870, the Monmouth Park Race-Course opened with great fanfare and a flurry of excitement as finely-dressed patrons entered the magnificent grandstand. Although the crowd on that balmy day was considerably smaller than anticipated, the inaugural meeting represented a milestone in New Jersey's turf history. Monmouth Park would elevate the "Sport of Kings" to new heights and establish unsurpassed standards of excellence.

A group of Long Branch hotel owners and entrepreneurs became concerned about the decline in tourism and decided that a racetrack would entice visitors back to the Jersey Shore. They needed to compete with other popular summertime resorts, especially New York's Saratoga. John Chamberlain, a wealthy New York businessman (and well-known gambler), the Honorable Amos Robins, President of the New Jersey Senate, and John Hoey, President of the Adams Express Company, were the leaders of the influential planners.

A mere three miles from the ocean watering place of Long Branch, the location of the one-mile course proved to be an excellent choice. The original 80-foot wide track, not to be confused with the present location of Monmouth Park in Oceanport, was situated on nearby land that is within the boundaries of Fort Monmouth in Eatontown. The entrance to the original track was located on what is now Broad Street near Park Avenue.

The first Monmouth Park meet in 1870 began with a hurdle race won by Lobelia. The entire race season that year lasted only five days. The "Continental Hotel Stakes" offered a purse of $800 and the featured race was the $1,000 Monmouth Stakes. The major hotels at "The Branch" sponsored races such as the "West End Hotel Stakes" and "Mansion House Stakes." Others were thanks to individuals such as Boss Tweed who donated money for The Tweed Purse.

In the early days, track patrons coming from New York would take the Naragansett Steamship Company's *Plymouth Rock* or *Jesse Hoyt*, from Pier 28 on the North River. They would land at Sandy Hook and then travel by train to Monmouth Park. After 1879, the track became more easily accessible to visitors who would

"The rush for the Long Branch Steamer - scene at Pier 27 in North River."
FRANK LESLIE'S ILLUSTRATED NEWSPAPER, JULY 26, 1873

This page from the log book of the PLYMOUTH ROCK possibly reflects the interest that gripped racing fans. On July 2, 1872 the steamer left New York at 11:45 A.M. and arrived at the Rail Road Wharf at Sandy Hook at 1:20. The only comments were : "W(ind) South West & moderate." Captain Tilton was in charge.
The return trip from Sandy Hook to New York was documented as follows: The Plymouth Rock left the Rail Road Wharf at 7:10 and arrived at New York at 9:00 P.M. The only comments were: "Capt. Tilton & Capt. Pearce went to horse Race & got left out."
Were they winners or losers?

Steamer PLYMOUTH ROCK,

From New York to Sandy Hook.

Stations.	Courses.	Watch Time.	Elapsed Time.	Tides.	Remarks.
New York,		1145		E	Date, July 2d 1872
Gov. Island,					W South West
Robins Reef,		126			& Moderate
Fort Tomkins,					
Buoy No. 13,					
Buoy No. 10½,					
Sandy Hook,					
R. R. Wharf.		120			
Running Time,	135				

From Sandy Hook to New York.

Stations.	Courses.	Watch Time.	Elapsed Time.	Tides.	Remarks.
R. R. Wharf,		710			Date, July 2d 1872
Sandy Hook,					Capt Tilton & Capt
Buoy No. 10½,					Pearce Went to horse
Buoy No. 13,					Race & got left out
Fort Tompkins,					
Robins Reef,					
Gov. Island,					
New York,		900			
Running Time,					

This 1870 advertisement for transportation between New York and Long Branch (via Sandy Hook) by the steamers PLYMOUTH ROCK and JESSE HOYT marks the beginning of an exciting season. At Sandy Hook, patrons transferred to the New Jersey Southern Railroad Line arriving at Long Branch via Highlands and Sea Bright. It was then another short ride to Monmouth Park. This was nine years before the Ocean Pier was built at Long Branch.

"Grandstand. Monmouth Park Race Track"

PACH STEREOGRAPH # 86, 1870

disembark from steamboats at the Branch's new Iron Pier, or from the nearby dock at Branchport. Efficient trains ran every half hour, starting at 10 a.m. to 3 p.m. from New York to Long Branch. Stories circulated about the unscrupulous, "rascally" local hack-drivers who eagerly picked up visitors as they arrived by boat or train. Outraged race track patrons accused the drivers of overcharging.

On Sunday, July 31, 1870, the day after Monmouth Park's opening, *THE NEW YORK TIMES* reported the event in detail on the front page:

> "The grandstand for spectators is probably the largest of any race-course in the United States. It is said to be capable of seating 6,000 people. It is surmounted by a Mansard roof, and presents a highly-ornamental appearance. The northern half is devoted to ladies accompanied by gentlemen, and was much more fully occupied yesterday than the southern half, allotted to the male solus..."

In the September 1876 edition of *HARPER'S NEW MONTHLY MAGAZINE*, popular author and theatrical personality Olive Logan wrote about life at Long Branch. Although somewhat subjective, her writing gives fascinating details about many activities including the race meets at Monmouth Park. According to Logan, ladies did not frequent the gambling houses with their roulette tables at the Branch, but going to the racetrack was accept-able behavior. "Those ladies who wish to indulge their passion for winning or losing at hazard can do so on stated days at Monmouth Park - a racing ground a short drive back in the country . . . " She goes on to comment that the races are managed by the same people who run the gambling houses at the Branch and there is a "club-house" apparently for men only. Some of her thoughts on the subject can best be appreciated in Olive Logan's flowery but lively writing style:

> "Fashion is a queer moralist; and the same people who would be horrified at the thought of joining the throng in Chamberlin club-house to toy with its tiger go without a qualm to the races at Monmouth Park, and bet their money on the running of horses instead of on the turning of a card. It is true that a large proportion of those who go to the races go as lovers of horseflesh, and never gamble there; but it is equally true that betting is freely and openly indulged in by many ladies as well as gentlemen who have been taught to look upon gambling as a terrible vice. Nor do they confine themselves to betting such trifles as gloves and bonbons, but boldly to win or lose hundreds of dollars. The system of 'mutual' pools, invented by the sporting men of Paris in connection with the races at Longchamps and Chantilly has been introduced at the Long Branch race-track within a year or two, and by it the number of bettors has been increased a hundredfold; for this system permits one to stake as small a sum

24

"Monmouth Park Club House"

Pach stereograph # 201, ca. 1871

LAYING WAGERS ON THE RACES
AT THE OCEAN HOTEL

It was not necessary to attend the races to "play the horses."
In the cool comfort of the OCEAN HOTEL's verandah, some fashionable women
appear to be very interested in "laying wagers on the races."

Frank Leslie's Illustrated Newspaper, July 24, 1880

as five dollars on a race, with a chance of winning something handsome."

Among the cigar-smoking gentlemen in top hats and ladies with parasols, an impressive array of celebrities attended the opening of Monmouth Park and notables could be seen every race day after that. Although President Ulysses S. Grant who summered in Long Branch did not appear at the inaugural of the track (according to *The New York Times*), he soon purchased a box. His presence increased the popularity of the attraction. Celebrated racetrack visitors from New York who generated excitement and whispers of scandal included Tammany Hall bosses and popular theatrical performers who frequented the Branch.

Horse racing is a spectator sport that attracts a variety of people from many different walks of life and has a long tradition in New Jersey making the state the home of many thoroughbred horse breeding farms. In 1665, Governor Nicholls, first Governor of New York and follower of King Charles II, made the first race track in America near Hempstead, Long Island, and called it "Newmarket" after the famous English course. Monmouth Park soon became known as "The

Newmarket of America" and "The Best Track in America." The racetrack was thriving during its early years and in 1872, a record crowd of 25,000 fans watched the historic match for the Monmouth Cup between thoroughbreds Harry Bassett, the East coast favorite, and Longfellow, the winner from Kentucky.

A syndicate headed by George L. Lorillard, D.D. Withers, G.P. Wetmore and James Gordon Bennett purchased Monmouth Park in 1878. They rekindled the spark and excitement of the track's opening by making improvements and offering handicaps and stakes including the famed Lorillard Stakes that attracted some of the fastest horses in the country.

Under Lorillard's leadership, the track became so successful that by 1889, the facility was bulging at its seams. Expansion to a larger site was the next step, and a new track emerged, reportedly the largest in the world then. The new Monmouth Park, slightly north of the old one, and about three times larger, opened on July 4, 1890. The newly-constructed course measured one and three-quarters miles in length, and the huge new grandstand, constructed entirely of iron, measured 700 feet long by 210 feet wide.

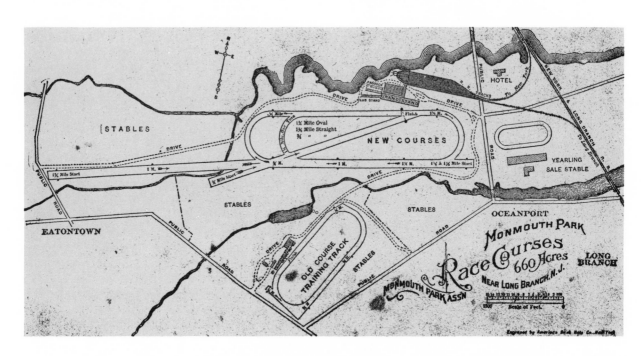

This map of the "New Monmouth Park Race Courses" shows the location and size
of the new (1890) track compared to the original one built in 1870.
MONMOUTH PARK ASSOCIATION BOOKLET, 1893

The new "Grandstand built on the cantilever truss system, Monmouth Park Race Course."
FRANK LESLIE'S POPULAR MONTHLY, SEPTEMBER, 1893

For women, a day at the horse races provided an exciting as well as a significant social event.
These are examples of both a "Lady's Season Ticket" and a "Lady's Club & Grand Stand" booklet for
Monmouth Park's season of 1892.

Unfortunately for Monmouth Park and to the detriment of the thriving hotel business at Long Branch, a powerful moralist movement led by James A. Bradley of Asbury Park to prohibit legalized gambling was gaining momentum. In 1894, legislation to stop gambling was passed in New Jersey. As a result, Monmouth Park shut down, and the facility fell into a sad state of disrepair.

The land that once housed the glorious old Monmouth Park was purchased by the United States Government in 1917 as the nation entered the World War. The former racetrack would be covered to make way for Camp Alfred Vail that was renamed Fort Monmouth in 1925.

The closing of the track and the lavish gambling clubs at the Branch came as a blow to the hotel owners, but they searched for creative ways to entertain their clientele. Entrepreneurs initiated all sorts of new activities. Elegant horse shows and dog shows became new events of great importance attracting well-to-do competitors and spectators from the cities. Boardwalk amusements, shops, and restaurants tried to fill the gaps, but the mood of the resort had changed.

On August 26, 1896, Phil Daly, who had owned a Long Branch gambling club, purchased property that was originally part of a larger tract of land owned by the Brinley family in the 1830s.

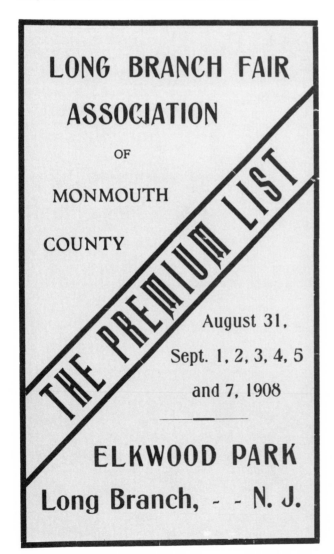

Elkwood Park later became the site of the current Monmouth Park. An event held there in 1908 was for the Long Branch Fair Association of Monmouth County.

THE RACING PROGRAM

MONDAY, AUGUST 31.

2.40 Class Trotting	$ 300
For horses owned in Monmouth and adjoining counties 30 days previous to race.	
2.25 Class Trotting	1,000
2.18 Class Pacing	1,000
2.12 Class Trotting	1,000
Running—5 furlongs for 2-year-olds	175

TUESDAY, SEPTEMBER 1.

2.30 Class Pacing	$ 300
For horses owned in Monmouth and adjoining counties 30 days previous to race.	
2.22 Class Pacing	1,000
2.18 Class Trotting	1,000
2.09 Class Pacing	1,000
Running—One mile	175

WEDNESDAY, SEPTEMBER 2.

2.21 Class Trotting	$1,000
2.13 Class Pacing	1,000
Free for All Trotting	1,000
Running—Five furlongs for Galloways	175

THURSDAY, SEPTEMBER 3.

2.07 Class Pacing	$1,000
2.15 Class Trotting	1,000
Free for All Pacing	1,000
Running—One mile and 70 yards	175

FRIDAY, SEPTEMBER 4.

2.15 Class Pacing	$1,000
2.10 Class Trotting	1,000
2.11 Class Pacing	1,000
Running—Five Furlongs	175

SATURDAY, SEPTEMBER 5.
All Running Races.

¼ Mile for Polo Ponies 14-2 and under, **Price Hotel Silver Cup**	
1 Mile and 70 yards	$175
4 Furlongs, for Ponies not over 14-2	175
Steeplechase, about 2 miles for the **Lewisohn Cup** and	175
5½ Furlongs for 2-year-olds	175
5½ Furlongs for Galloways 15 hands and under	175

MONDAY, SEPTEMBER 7.

¼ Mile, for Polo Ponies 14-2 and under, The **Pannaci Hotel of Long Branch Silver Cup.**	
1 Mile and 70 yards	$175
4 Furlongs, for Ponies not over 14-2	175
Steeplechase, about 2 miles	
for The **Long Branch Fair Association Silver Cup.**	
5½ Furlongs for 2-year-olds	175
5½ Furlongs for Galloways, 15 hands and under	175

Page 55 of the Program listed the Races. One of the prizes, on September 7th, was the Pannaci Hotel of Long Branch Silver Cup.

LONG BRANCH FAIR ASSOCIATION PROGRAM, ELKWOOD PARK, 1908

On this tract of land in Oceanport (site of the present Monmouth Park Racetrack) Daly built Elkwood Park which included a race track as part of its attractions. In 1901, a number of sportsmen formed a corporation called "The Gentlemen's Driving and Field Club of Monmouth County." Its principal office was at Elkwood Park. The main purposes of the Club included holding "exhibitions of speed, races and meetings of horses" and "to offer prizes money and rewards at such exhibitions and competition."

In 1905, Walter Lewisohn became one of the new owners. Elkwood Park offered space for many leisure time events including horseracing without wagering, and automobile racing. The park included a twelve-room house, an eight room guest cottage, a casino with a ballroom and other buildings.

A popular event in September of 1908 at Elkwood Park was the spectacular Long Branch Fair of Monmouth County. During its seven-day duration, an incredible number of livestock, agricultural examples and Ladies' Art and Fancy Work were judged. The horse racing program offered about five competitive events each day. Hotels still supported these events. A quarter of a mile race, for example, was for the Pannaci Hotel of Long Branch Silver Cup.

In the early 1920s, the Ku Klux Klan used Elkwood Park for both official meetings and various recreational activities. On June 20, 1924, J. William Jones and Oliver G. Frake acquired most of Elkwood Park. Interestingly, this purchase was made just a few weeks before the Klan's huge "Tri-State Konklave," was held there on July 4, 1924. On November 16, 1925, Jones and Frake, sold the property to the Elkwood Park Association of Long Branch.

For over fifty years, wagering on horses was not allowed in New Jersey until Amory L. Haskell lobbied to legalize parimutal wagering in the 1940s. Finally, a new Monmouth Park held its first race on June 19, 1946, at the Oceanport location where the state-of-the-art track operates today and draws large crowds to the Long Branch area. The cry, "And they're off!" echoes the past as horse racing at Monmouth Park continues into the 21st century.

A Grand Stand ticket for the first racing day at the "new" Monmouth Park in June of 1946.

"Bathing in the shade beneath the pier." This scene captures the spirit of a refreshing summer's day at Long Branch. Inquisitive visitors on the pier are observing the activities of bathers in the rolling surf below. Also on the pier, at the extreme left, is a cannon often used to salute incoming vessels. In the distance, the PLYMOUTH ROCK *can be seen maneuvering for a landing.*

FRANK LESLIE'S ILLUSTRATED NEWSPAPER, AUGUST 23, 1879

An artist's rendering of the Ocean Pier showing its location in front of the Ocean Hotel. The illustration also depicts other hotels along the bluff south of the new pier.
HARPER'S WEEKLY, JUNE 21, 1879

The Ocean Piers

In the summer of 1879, a newly-built ocean pier at Long Branch quickly became known as "the stepping stone to the Jersey Shore." For many summer visitors who travelled by steamboat for the first time from New York to this popular seaside resort, the pier was an impressive landmark. Visitors already enjoying their summer holiday at the shore also found it a delightful place to meet and socialize.

Little is known of the history of the first ocean pier at Long Branch. Called the Bath House Pier, it was built in 1828 at the foot of Bath Avenue. The same storm responsible for the wreck of the sailing ship *New Era* (and the loss of 240 lives) in November of 1854 near what later became Asbury Park also destroyed this pier.

The second structure, the EAST END EXCURSION PAVILION, had a rather short life. A newspaper article, in May of 1875, indicated that it was possibly built by Jay Gould who was involved in the EAST END HOUSE. This hotel, originally the ATLANTIC HOTEL located just north of Troutman Avenue, became the ARLINGTON HOUSE and for a few weeks was known as the LONG BRANCH EXCURSION HOUSE before it was renamed the EAST END HOUSE. In referring to the EAST END EXCURSION PAVILION the reporter stated in Victorian prose:

"The principle of construction of this pier is not unlike that of the bridge which Caesar built over the Rhine in days when Ariovistus had no Bismark to keep watch over it. The pine logs which are used as supports are driven...with a

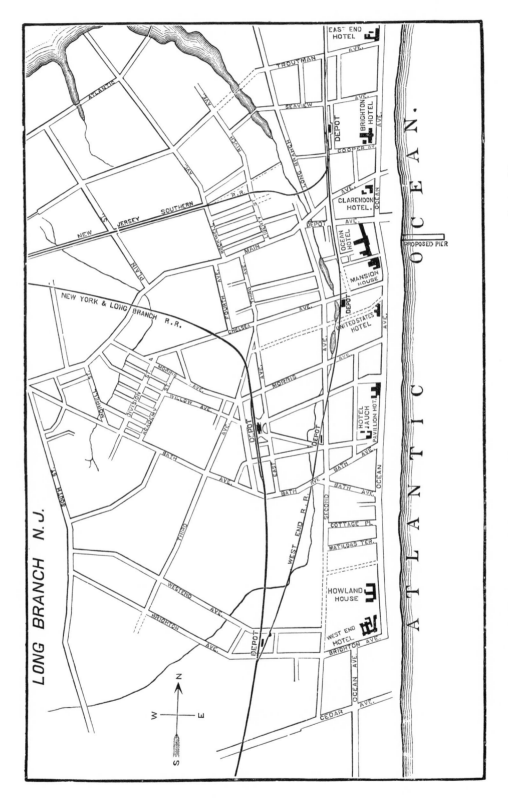

This map of Long Branch identifies ten hotels located on Ocean Avenue as depicted in "Summer Excursion Routes, Season of 1879" published by the Pennsylvania Railroad Company. The map also identifies the "proposed pier."

32

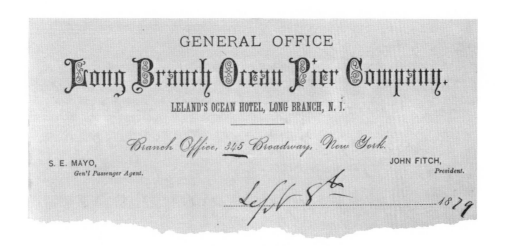

The Long Branch Ocean Pier Company's letterhead indicates that the General Office was actually in LELAND'S OCEAN HOTEL *opposite the Pier.*

SEPTEMBER 8, 1879

A rare stock certificate representing four shares of the Long Branch Ocean Pier Company. In the center of this stock certificate is a beautiful engraving of the original Ocean Pier depicting a vessel about to make a landing.

AUGUST 13, 1889

pile driver that weighs a thousand pounds, and makes the frail structure jump every time it descends. It really does not look as if it would stand a high tide and a strong gale from the east... This pier is so very narrow that it can only serve as a landing place for excursion steamers, and even the ladies will hardly care to walk upon it. As for a promenade, that is out of the question."[1]

When finished, true to these comments, the pier lasted little more than a week before it was demolished by a violent storm.

In 1878, the Long Branch Pier Association decided to erect their own ocean pier. The impressive tubular iron structure was designed by a major stockholder from Brooklyn, Mr. Job Johnson. Early in the following summer, the New York engineering firm of G. W. Maclay and W. E. Davies (who constructed a similar Iron Pier at Coney Island) built this new Long Branch pier.

The first reference to the proposed pier appeared in a Pennsylvania Railroad publication in the beginning of 1879:

> "The site of Long Branch is upon a bluff twenty feet high, upon the edge of which is constructed the grand drive five miles in length. One hundred feet back are located the hotels, from the porches of which may be seen showy equipages, in passing and repassing lines,

pleasantly breaking the vision of the bright green of the lawn and the deep blue of the ocean beyond. There are at Long Branch no salt marches, sandy plains, nor mosquitoes. The soil from the bluff back is one of the most fertile character, and the art of man working upon this and aided by unlimited capital has done so much to beautify the place and add to the great natural attraction of the sea that it can never be in any danger of losing its high rank and prestige. A magnificent wrought-iron tubular pier, extending six hundred and sixty feet into the ocean, will be completed and ready for use for the season of 1879. It will constitute a splendid promenade, and be utilized for various purposes, which will make it a most important novelty, and add materially to the fame and popularity of Long Branch."[2]

Called the Ocean Pier, it was erected opposite stockholder Warren Leland's OCEAN HOTEL, the largest summer hotel in the United States at that time. The Long Branch Ocean Pier Company actually had its main office in the hotel. Projecting more than 600 feet into the Atlantic, the Ocean Pier soon was one of the major attractions at the "Branch." It truly became the "stepping stone to the Jersey Shore" and soon became a positive force in the growth of the local economy.

Docking facilities allowed popular steamers including the *Adelaide, Plymouth Rock, City of Richmond, Cygnus, Taurus* and *Columbia* to even-

The ADELAIDE arriving at the south side of the new Ocean Pier.
PACH STEREOGRAPH #LBU604C, 1879

An early view of "Leland's Gun" shows its location on the bluff. In the background is the left wing of the OCEAN HOTEL. The left wing was originally CONGRESS HALL and became part of the large CONTINENTAL HOTEL (later named LELAND'S OCEAN HOTEL).

PACH STEREOGRAPH #193, 1873

This view of the Ocean Pier shows the steamer PLYMOUTH ROCK about to dock on the north side of the pier. The direction of the wind was the deciding factor as to which side of the pier a vessel would dock.

PACH STEREOGRAPH #605A, 1879

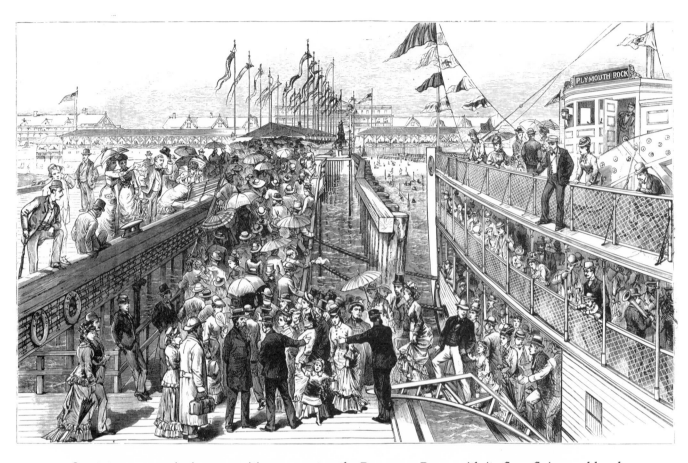

Spectators were enjoying an exciting moment as the PLYMOUTH ROCK, with its flags flying and band playing, finally docked and discharged equally excited passengers at the new Ocean Pier.

FRANK LESLIE'S ILLUSTRATED NEWSPAPER, AUGUST 23, 1879

tually bring thousands of passengers back and forth from New York to Long Branch. Even though not yet completed, the pier opened for business on June 14, 1879. The 734 ton excursion steamer *Adelaide* carried more than 650 excited visitors to the Branch that day.

To commemorate that first landing, a cannon was fired in celebration as hundreds of spectators cheered. Known as both "Leland's Gun" and "Old Monmouth," it was situated in front of Leland's OCEAN HOTEL and often used to salute other pass-

ing vessels. Another cannon, located at the end of the pier, was also often fired to announce the arrival of an incoming vessel.

A week after the first landing of the *Adelaide* the 1,752 ton steamer *Plymouth Rock* arrived with 1,600 excursionists. They enjoyed just one hour on the beach and then embarked for their return voyage to New York via Rockaway. There, they enjoyed one more stroll on another beach before re-embarking for their final return to lower Manhattan.

PLYMOUTH ROCK

—FOR—

LONG BRANCH

DIRECT TO THE MAMMOTH WROUGHT IRON TUBULAR

OCEAN PIER.

Time Table No. 1, Commencing July 1st, 1880.

TWO TRIPS DAILY, INCLUDING SUNDAYS.

—:o:—

Leave New York

Foot W. 22d St., N. Y., 9.30 A. M. and 2.45 P. M.
Stone Pier, No. 1, N. R., 10.00 A. M. and 3.15 P. M.

Returning Leave Long Branch

From Ocean Pier, 12.15 P. M. and 6.25 P. M.

BENT'S CELEBRATED MARINE BAND !
CANTERBURY CATHEDRAL CHIME OF CHURCH BELLS !
WONDERFUL ELECTRIC LIGHT !
DELIGHTFUL OCEAN SAIL !
UNSURPASSED SURF BATHING !
IMPROVED BATHING HOUSES !
SPLENDID DRIVES ! ELEGANT PROMENADES !
And the PIONEER OCEAN PIER of America are among the attractions at this
FAMOUS WATERING PLACE.

FARE, (either way, including Pier,) **50 CENTS.**

EXCURSION TICKETS, good only on day sold and including Pier admissions, - **60 CENTS.**

An advertising card for the 1,752 ton Plymouth Rock. *This 330 foot steamboat was the largest vessel to carry passengers between New York and the great pier at Long Branch. Besides the* Plymouth Rock's *timetable, the card also noted some of "the attractions at this FAMOUS WATERING PLACE."*

Plymouth Rock Advertising Card, July 1880

From illustrations of the period (photographic as well as artistic engravings), it is obvious the Ocean Pier soon became a center of pleasant social activities: a place to see and be seen, a place to converse in the shade with friends and to observe the newest arrivals and the latest fashions.

Just a week before the Ocean Pier opened for use in June of 1879, a comment in *Frank Leslie's Illustrated Newspaper* anticipated the social impact of this new attraction:

> "..settees were placed for the accommodation of visitors, who, from the elevation of the pier, and several hundred feet from the shore, could enjoy the ocean breeze and indulge in reading or dreaming, with the most exquisite sense of exhilaration."[3]

By July of 1879, the summer season at Long Branch was in full swing. To appreciate the interest and the novelty of the pier, on July 4th, just a few weeks after it opened, more than 7,000 people paid 10 cents for admission just to walk upon the yet unfinished structure. According to a *New York Times* correspondent:

> "..in one way the proposed speedy completion of the pier will not prove entirely satisfactory. There is now 260 feet of the outer pier unrailed and unlighted. When the shades of evening fall, hundreds of spoony couples hie themselves, carrying surreptitious stools, which they plant in obscure corners. There they sit for hours, whispering together so softly that the stranger strolling seaward is astonished to see their still figures looming up indistinctly out of the darkness at every point. Next week there will remain many cozy nooks in which soft nothings may be whispered, but under the glare on the gaslights the lovers will be compelled to sit wider apart."[4]

So much for progress!

A major December snow storm and extreme winds in 1880 unfortunately demolished this popular pier. However, in 1881 a new ocean pier quickly replaced the previous one. Even though named the Iron Pier, the new structure was often referred to by both names: the Ocean Pier or the Iron Pier as evidenced by various advertisements of the period.

While the new Iron Pier appears to have been built in the same location as the old Ocean Pier, its entrance was north in a Pavilion at the foot of South Broadway. The Pavilion ran south on the bluff for about 300 feet and, at that point, the pier extended into the Atlantic Ocean almost from the exact location of the previous structure.

The following description, taken from an 1881 publication, almost fits both piers.

The boardwalk in front of the entrance to the Ocean Pier was equally popular. Crowds were attracted as many public activities took place nearby including reviewing of troops and band concerts.

PACH STEREOGRAPH #603A, 1879

"One of the latest features of Long Branch is the new iron pier, extending from the bluff out into the ocean over 800 feet. It reaches far beyond the breakers, and its top is on a level with the bluff. It is supported by numerous hollow wrought-iron piles, a foot in diameter, driven into the sand many feet, and bound together by at top by immense iron girders. It is immediately opposite the main front entrance of the Ocean Hotel.It is intended to afford opportunity for landing passengers and freight by boat. On its top is a restaurant, accommodations for an orchestra, and a long promenade, and from it fishing may be indulged. Underneath it are the numerous bath-houses of the Ocean Hotel."[5]

The significance of the new Iron Pier's attraction to nearby local business establishments was reflected in numerous newspaper advertisements.

In 1881, for example, the owner of KOLB'S HOTEL, an extremely small establishment (more Restaurant than Hotel and west of Ocean Avenue along the north side of South Broadway) took advantage of this location. J. V. Kolb's advertisements often mentioned that his Hotel and Restaurant were "Opposite the Iron Pier."

THE LONG BRANCH RECORD on August 7, 1886, carried another typical advertisement stating that Kolb's Hotel and Restaurant, still on the European Plan, was opposite the Ocean Hotel and the Great Iron Pier. Regular dinner, by the way, was offered from 12 to 4 P.M. and cost only 75 cents. Kolb died in 1900 and the hotel was subsequently sold.

In 1893, the pier was severely damaged by a dramatic tug boat accident. Much of it had to be replaced and it was unlike the previous pier. In fact a scathing article appeared that same year in *THE LONG BRANCH RECORD* which painted quite a different picture of what the Branch was like at this particular period in time.

"It was once considered the salvation of Long Branch - but proved its death. The Ocean Pier, at this place, which was built in 1878, will be torn down and sold for old iron. This is rather a sad ending of what was at one time thought to be an institution that would make Long Branch unique and raise it to greater popularity. Great things were expected of the Iron Pier but great disappointments have been the reward of the confident stockholders. The Pier has never had a financial success. It had several prosperous seasons but they were more

MENU.

SOUPS
Mock Turtle.   Chicken, Consommé

FISH.
Filet of Sea Bass, à la Hollandaise.
Bluefish, Maitre d'Hotel,
Potatoes, Parisienne.

RELISHES,
Raw Tomatoes.   Olives.   Radishes

ENTREES.
Tenderloin of Beef, Mushroom Sauce,
Lamb Crops, with French Peas.

ENTREMET.
Asparagus, Butter sauce.

ROAST.
Spring Chicken, with Lettuce.

Chicken Salad.   Lobster Salad.

DESSERT.
Neapolitan Ice Cream.
Mixed Cakes.   Bon Bons.
Mottoes—variety.
Fruit.
Coffee.

KOLB'S HOTEL,   LONG BRANCH.

This menu from Kolb's Restaurant was typical of what one could expect. The food was basic but tasty and very well prepared. It satisfied many visitors season after season.
COURTESY OF JOAN C. MEEHAN

than overbalanced by several seasons of storm when the Pier was greatly damaged. The Lelands, who then owned the OCEAN HOTEL, were large stockholders in the enterprise and they were confident that the Pier would add to the popularity of their hotel.

In this they were wrong. The people that came on the boats swarmed into the OCEAN HOTEL monopolized the piazza and converted the place into a pic-nic resort. Of course this was distasteful to the Hotel guests and many families who had been spending their summer for years with the Lelands and went to the WEST END (HOTEL) to escape the rabble which the Pier boats discharged twice a day.

That the Pier has been a great detriment to the north end of the town no one who has watched the decline of real estate values and of tone in the vicinity of the Pier will deny. Beer shops sprung up like mushrooms to cater to the people who came on the boats. Petty gambling dens and catch penny institutions of all kinds took up their abode in what was once the Helmbold Block and many of them are there

still. The Ocean Pier is a failure and in going down it has dragged a portion of our town with it. It will take years for Long Branch to recover from the scars inflicted by the Pier and its influences."[6]

There is no doubt that by the 1890s there was more leisure time for the general public and less of the rather exclusive social life that existed in the past. As society changed, more crowds of visitors came to the shore just for a day's visit. Long Branch was not quite the same as it was in the glory days of the 1870s.

In time the New York steamboats were phased out and by 1908 the remains of the old pier were finally torn down. By 1912, a smaller scale amusement pier was built in its place. Noted for its many games, marathon dancing, rides and fishing facilities for decades, this popular pier (with a number of changes) was ultimately destroyed by a spectacular fire in 1987. The unsightly ruins were finally removed in the beginning of 1998. A sixth ocean pier has been under consideration.

In the style of the "GRAND HOTELS," this invitation was offered to guests of Kolb's Hotel to attend a complimentary Hop on August 4, 1880. Kolb's Hotel Restaurant had quite a following.

COURTESY OF JOAN C. MEEHAN

IAUCH'S HOTEL   UNITED STATES HOTEL   MANSION HOUSE   METROPOLITAN HOTEL

CENTRAL HOTEL   OCEAN HOTEL   EAST END HOTEL

LONG BRANCH, FROM THE SEA.—[From Sketches by Theo. R. Davis.]

WEST END HOTEL   HOWLAND HOUSE

This is only a **partial** list of the many hotels and boarding houses that existed (from south to north) on Ocean Avenue, Long Branch, between 1800 and 1900. The "grand hotels" are identified by number.

Lawn House. Built 1832 became *Conover House* until 1865. Torn down.

1- *STETSON HOUSE.*
Built 1866 on site. Became *WEST END HOTEL* in 1870. Torn down 1906.

2- *HOWLAND HOUSE.*
Built 1851. Storm damaged 1902. Eventually torn down. Contents sold 1906.

Bath Hotel. Burned 1867.

Scarboro. Built 1882.

3- *IAUCH'S HOTEL.*
Built 1868 became *PANNACI HOTEL* 1897. Torn down 1932.

Pavilion Hotel. Built 1851.

Atlantic Hotel. Built 1880. Burned 1927.

4- *UNITED STATES HOTEL.*
Built 1852 became *PITMAN HOUSE* in 1868 became *UNITED STATES HOTEL* again.

5- *CENTRAL HOTEL.*
Built 1873. Burned by 1877.

6- *MORRIS HOUSE.*
Built 1846 became *MANSION HOUSE* 1852.

Cooper Boarding House. Built 1840 became *National House.*

Congress Hall.

7 -The above two hotels (*National House* and *Congress Hall*) connected by a center wing became The *CONTINENTAL HOTEL* 1866 and later became the *OCEAN HOTEL* 1872. Closed 1902. Torn down by 1906.

Lanes End. Built ca. 1800 replaced by *Clarendon* 1836.

Ocean Wave (possibly the *Clarendon*).

8- *METROPOLITAN.* Built 1854.
Burned 1876.

9- *BRIGHTON.*
Built on site of **METROPOLITAN** 1878. Later became the *Ambassador.* Burned 1930.

10- *ATLANTIC HOTEL.* Built 1861. Became the *ARLINGTON* then became the *GRAND EXCURSION HOUSE* then became the *EAST END.*
Storm damaged. Torn down in 1881.

For a view of the Long Branch hotels on the bluff in 1873, open this foldout. ⟶

"Long Branch From the West" is a revealing inland view of some of the hotels and cottages along busy Ocean Avenue. It also captures the vast rural scene that existed behind those buildings during the early years.

APPLETON'S JOURNAL, SEPTEMBER 7, 1872

The Grand Hotels

For more than a century, a vast number of boarding houses and hotels were built in Long Branch. However, recognizing the advantages of the invigorating ocean breeze, the beach, and the magnificent view of the sea from the bluff, the "grandest" hotels were ultimately built just along Ocean Avenue. The hotels documented in this book were selected because of the significant role they played in the social world of the Victorian era at the Jersey Shore.

These hotels are not listed chronologically, but are presented according to their individual locations on Ocean Avenue from south to north — from Brighton Avenue to Troutman Avenue (now Joline Avenue). Even though all of these hotels did not exist at the same time, the pages that follow will help create for the reader a clearer mental picture of those Victorian Summers at Long Branch. The talented writers and artists who were there provide an intimate glimpse into the past and prove that, through changing times, nothing remains the same.

MOST RESPECTFULLY DEDICATED TO CHARLES A STETSON JR. ESQ.

THE STETSON HOUSE LANCERS.

AS PERFORMED WITH GREAT SUCCESS AT LONG BRANCH,
BY
GILMORE'S CELEBRATED BAND
OF BOSTON
COMPOSED BY

FERDINAND ZOEHLER,

OF GILMORES BAND.

BOSTON:
Published by **W. H. CUNDY.** 1195 Washington St.

| BOSTON, | NEW YORK. | CHICAGO. | PHILADELPHIA. |
| H. TOLMAN & CO. | W A POND. | ROOT & CADY. | LEE & WALKER. |

This illustration is from the cover of a musical number entitled "The Stetson House Lancers,"
which was dedicated to Charles A. Stetson Jr, the proprietor of the newly-built Stetson House.
One of the earliest illustrations of the hotel, it also shows a midday concert in progress -
possibly under the direction of band leader Gilmore (ca. 1867).

COURTESY OF PHIL DELCAMP

A view of the east or Ocean Avenue side of the West End Hotel.
The hotel's own fancy white carriage, filled with passengers, can be seen in the center of the photograph.
PACH STEREOGRAPH #59, CA. 1874

Stetson House – West End Hotel

The STETSON HOUSE, later The WEST END HOTEL, was the most southern of the grand hotels. It was located on the corner of Brighton and Ocean Avenues, formerly the site of a farm house built for Cornelius Lane in 1832. The house was enlarged and named the LAWN HOUSE and became the first hotel to occupy that location. In 1835 the building was sold along with fifty acres for $5,000 to John V. Conover and renamed the CONOVER HOUSE. It had a capacity for 175 guests by 1851.

In 1865, the property was then purchased by the Astor House Hotel Company for $60,000. Although a small portion of the original building was retained, a much larger 300 room edition was added. Under the proprietorship of Charles A. Stetson Jr., this new hotel, now called the STETSON HOUSE, opened for business on June 21, 1866.

"...the STETSON HOUSE celebrated its opening in an appropriate and festive manner. Every arrangement had been made to conduce to the comfort and pleasure of the guests, and render the occasion one long to be remembered.

Co. A, 71st New York Militia, accepted the invitation of the Stetsons, to make this, the fortieth anniversary of the Light Guard, the occasion for formally throwing open the spacious rooms of the STETSON HOUSE to the public.

The military arrived in the 11 o'clock A.M. Train, on the Raritan & Delaware Bay Railroad, and preceded by D. L. Downing's full regimental band of twenty pieces, marched to the STETSON HOUSE.

Upon arriving at the STETSON, the company broke ranks, and after a few minutes of rest and refreshments, again formed, and occupied about an hour in target practice.

At 2 o'clock, dinner was announced, when Co. A filed into the spacious dining room, followed by the invited guests. The bill of fare was such as would tempt the palate of the most fastidious epicure, and was done justice to by the 'boys' of Co. A."[1]

By opening day, the STETSON HOUSE was almost filled to capacity with 102 pre-registered families. It was a gala event for all of Long Branch and attracted hundreds of interested visitors. The first review of the hotel appeared in a local newspaper and reads in part.

"The building is three stories high, with four turrets rising above the roof, and in each turret are eight rooms. It is in the form of an L., the short angle facing east, being 250 front, and the long and main front and entrance 362 feet facing south, making an aggregate length of building and portico of 612 feet.

There are 250 chambers, and twenty private parlors, and there are upwards of forty miles of bell wire distributed through the house. There are gas and bells in every room. There are bathrooms, and every other convenience, on every floor, that is to be found in the most fashionable modern hotels...."

Additional comments from this article are both humorous and serious.

"...here is an innovation on old established principles. Where are the porticos to the upper stories? I have heard the case of portico vs. no portico very much discussed of late. The subject has exercised the gossips greatly, and I confess my own mind was somewhat befogged about their relative merits, until a few evenings, I heard a lady's opinion on the subject, and she made a convert of me on the spot - She said balconies are a nuisance; ladies do not want to be stayed and hooped into shape all the time; they like to take their ease as well as the men; they want occasionally to unlace their corsets and lounge about in dishabille; where there are balconies you cannot do it without letting down the windows and closing the shutters, and even then some prying puppy will be trying to peek through the blinds, and no matter how hot the night may be, you must keep them closed, even at the risk of suffocation. But when there are no balconies, you may sleep with your windows open, regardless of sneaking and prying puppies or impertinent staring ones. That's a clear case and I give a verdict in favor of the lady's opinion."[2]

Speaking of "stayed and hooped," it appears that some young ladies occasionally had problems with that particular style of attire. An item of interest that was undoubtedly read by many guests of the Hotel appeared in the LONG BRANCH NEWS in the summer of 1866. This incident allegedly happened in New York City at Broadway and Liberty Street.

"Six handsome and stylish young ladies were waiting for a Madison Avenue stage...and as the street was crowded with vehicles, it was very important that they should get into the vehicle as fast as possible. As the first young lady, about eighteen summers, entered the narrow stage door, out sprang her immense "tilte," and the second young lady with a charming little "Stella" hat on her bewitching frizzled hair in her great haste to follow, ran up under the hoops and was dragged forward, while the third young lady got enveloped in like manner and so on until all had rushed in, pell-mell, under each others hoops, in less time than it takes to tell it. The horses having started suddenly, precipitated them like so many bricks, one knocking the other over. It was indeed a ludicrous sight. But as the ladies were all alone, they did not seem to be embarrassed at their situation. The ladies succeeded in disentangling themselves without serious injury."[3]

So much for the perils of the fashions of the day.

The STETSON HOUSE quickly became a popular destination at Long Branch as it offered all the amenities summer visitors expected at a vacation resort. Superb food and diverse social events more than pleased most of the patrons.

A hop or a grand ball was, typically, a very social evening and a great source of entertainment and merriment for those staying at almost any hotel at the Branch. Each establishment, in its own way, was noted for glamour and excitement at those special evenings. The exceptional quality of music that was offered at various times throughout the day was considered a bonus. On July 4, 1866, the STETSON HOUSE held one of those special evening events.

First "...the guests thronged the parlors, and promenades, to witness the fine display of fireworks which the Messrs. Stetsons had provided for the occasion. The closing piece was especially worthy of remark; it represented an eagle, with extended wings under it the magic talisman in variegated colors "Union." the fireworks drew repeated applause from the spectators, and was certainly well managed.

A band discoursed excellent music during the evening, and the light-footed dancers waltzed through the "giddy maze of the dance," keeping time to the cadence of the

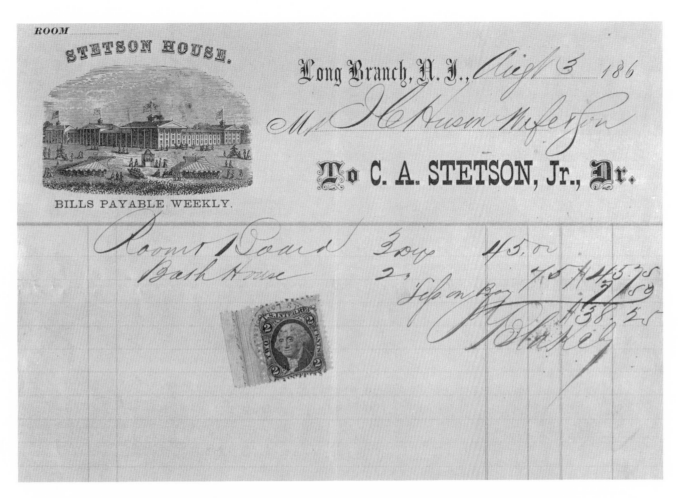

This bill from the STETSON HOUSE dated August 3, 1868, was for room and board covering a three-day stay and use of a Bath House for a family of three.

spirit-stirring melody. At 11 o'clock the guests repaired to the dinning hall for refreshments, and again resumed the "hop," and not until the "wee sma' hours of the morn" did the pleasant company separate, to find repose."[4]

On one occasion the STETSON HOUSE became the center stage for a grand ball given in honor of President Ulysses S. Grant. This was a singularly hot and suffocating evening in July of 1869. Reports from the press appeared in print shortly thereafter.

"A fashionable ball at Long Branch is always a great event. There are half a dozen or more hotels filled with the votaries of fashion, who come to the beach not for health, not for the relief from the tumult of city life, so much as because there they find a new field for display, a fresh season of excitement. Now a grand ball, under these circumstances, is just the thing. Hotel-keepers enjoy it, for they make money out of it. The ladies enjoy it, because they have an opportunity to show themselves "at their prettiest" with their splendid dresses and costly diamonds. The gentlemen enjoy it in a lazy sort of way, especially if they are rich, or handsome, or can appear upon the committee list.

The fashionable world has its competitions, and they are not less acrimonious or less interesting to those engaged in them than are the strife politicians. Many a dandy prides himself as much upon his spotless white vest or his graceful dancing. And do you suppose that the gentlemen upon the "Ball Committee" or the "Floor Committee" would change places, even if they were offered positions on the Congressional Reconstruction Committee? We doubt it.

It can be imagined, then, what excitement was occasioned by the announcement of a ball at Long Branch, on the evening of July 26, in honor of President Grant. The event took place at the STETSON HOUSE, and the entire establishment was devoted to it. It was a grand affair. The President, of course was there; and there were ex-Secretary Borie, General Sherman, Gen-

*"Grand Ball given in honor of President Grant at the STETSON HOUSE,
Long Branch, July 26 – Drawn by C. G. Bush."*

HARPER'S WEEKLY, AUGUST 14, 1869

eral Sheridan, and other prominent personages. The grounds about the hotel were illuminated with calcium lights, and the stream of fashion poured endlessly on and emptied itself out at the doors of the STETSON HOUSE."

An illustration accompanying the above article portrayed President Grant dancing with Mrs. Borie while others joined in, including

"...General Sheriden with General Sherman's daughter, General Sherman with Mrs. Grant and General Comstock with his wife. After this dance President Grant became a martyr, as he has so often done before, and shook hands with about four hundred of the guests. Then the dance went on again. The President retired to a sofa, but General Sheriden took part in every dance. About midnight supper was served on a table 190 feet in length. The most prominent of the guests then retired, but others returned to the festive dance, and kept it up til morning."[5]

So why was there not a smile to be seen on a single face at this delightful event? Considering the crowded room, the extreme heat of the night, the heavy military uniforms of the men and the voluminous attire of the women - it was hardly a joyous moment.

Two of the ladies can be seen carrying their own nosegays perhaps hoping to add a little freshness to the stifling and stagnant air. It was not uncommon for these social hops to continue until morning. After all, it was the type of entertainment that the patrons adored (even though there were those uncomfortable moments) and the dance was no doubt a subject of conversation for many days to come.

50

"President Grant at Long Branch - the President and his party enjoying a bath in the surf."
FRANK LESLIE'S ILLUSTRATED NEWSPAPER, AUG. 7, 1869

President Grant also was involved in many other enjoyable activities at the Branch. In this illustration, a few weeks after the previously mentioned ball, he is seen taking advantage of one of the more exhilarating sports of the day. From the artist's rendering, it appears the young man on the President's shoulders was not too overjoyed to be particpating in "surfing" at this moment.

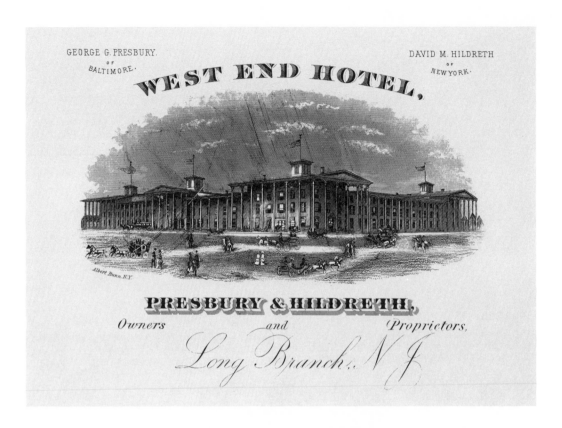

An engraved advertisement for the WEST END HOTEL displaying the names of Presbury and Hildreth, the newest "Owners and Proprietors" of that establishment, ca. 1875.

Frequent changes of ownership were common in the hotel industry. By 1870, this large hotel was sold to Sykes, Gardner & Company and renamed the WEST END HOTEL. By 1872 Presbury & Sykes were owners and a few years later Presbury & Hildreth became the owners and proprietors.

About $120,000 was spent on improvements, a considerable amount of money in those days. By 1878, among the important improvements to the hotel were...

"...an additional building, a new stable, a hydraulic passenger elevator (the only one on the shore), a laundry on the premise where 10,000 pieces have been turned out in a day; two separate gas works, forming an immunity against failure; a bath building adjoining the hotel, drawing sea water from 200 yards out in the sea, heating 50,000 gallons at a time and furnishing it hot or cold in 50 separate bath rooms. Mr. Presbury formerly was proprietor of Willard's at Washington, and presides over the comfort of his guests with the genial dignity of a gentlemen of the olden time."[6]

"The WEST END HOTEL, the gem of Long Branch, is the dwelling place of the elite. It has a frontage of 750 feet, L-shaped, and with all modern improvements, including electric bells, gas, bath-rooms, etc. The dining-room is 120 by 60 feet, and the office, reception rooms, and parlors are superior to those of any hotel at Long Branch.

Ernest Neyer's Orchestra furnished the music, and the obliging proprietors, Messrs. Presbury and Hildreth, pay for it.

The Bill of Fare of the WEST END is not only a beautiful specimen of engraving, but suggests every delicacy of the season, all of which are served bountifully.

All the pretty girls are to be seen here, and it requires strong nerves for an unprotected man to walk through the ball-room and over

These two spoons are examples from the STETSON HOUSE and the WEST END HOTEL. The STETSON HOUSE spoon dates from around 1866. The WEST END spoon dates from around 1872.

When the STETSON HOUSE was sold and renamed the WEST END HOTEL, it was important that the name on the silverware be immediately changed. This example shows the first hurried effort to make that change which was simply stamping the new name over the old one. This spoon dates from 1870.

the piazza in the full blaze of female beauty which is visible every night. There is no extra charge for all this show. The proprietors are liberal, and will take only $5 per day.

Mr. Farrah of Saratoga and Mr. W. Edgar Wooley, are the clerks.

The WEST END is one of the most imposing and stylish hotels at the Branch. It was built for the Stetsons of the ASTOR HOUSE, New York, but who failed to make it a paying institution. It is situated about one mile from the station and village, and is the farthermost boundary of the mammoth caravansaries for which the watering place is noted, and can accommodate nicely 800 guests.

The clerks of the WEST END are among the most polished gentlemen in their department we have ever met, and the guests of the WEST END receive every comfort and attention."[7]

A young child sits all alone at a table in the beautiful and spacious parlor of the WEST END HOTEL.
PACH STEREOGRAPH #140, CA. 1874

DINNER.

WEST END HOTEL, SUNDAY, JULY 26, 1903

Little Neck Clams

SOUP.

Green Turtle à l'Anglaise   Consommé Ab-del-Kader

HORS D'OEUVRES.

Saucisson d'Arle

Olives   Celery   Chow Chow

FISH.

Boiled Kennebec Salmon Choisseuil

Broiled Spanish Mackerel Sauce Preau-Vert   Pommes Frissard

RELEVE.

Baked Pork and Beans   Vermont Turkey, Sauce Suprême

ENTREES.

Tenderloin of Beef Piqué Chatillon Plessis

Sweetbreads en Cassolette à la Marin

Chicken Patties Dame Blanche

Baked Apples à la Reine

ROAST.

Prime Ribs of Beef au jus   Maryland Ham, Sauce fine Champagne

Young Duckling, Apple Sauce   Spring Chicken, Giblet Sauce

Pain de Foie Gras Périgourdine

SALAD.

Lobster Mayonnaise   Lettuce   Tomato   Cresson

VEGETABLES.

Mashed Potatoes   Boiled Potatoes   Baked Potatoes

Stewed Tomatoes   Steamed Rice

Butter Beets Sauté   Green Corn   New Peas a l'anglaise

PASTRY.

Cabinet Pudding, Brandy Sauce

Raspberry Meringne Pie   Peach Pie   Petits Fours   Citron Cake

Assorted Fancy Cakes   Rhine Wine Jelly   Pistache Ice Cream

DESSERT.

Oanges   Watermelon   Bananas   Raisins

Pecans   Almonds

English Walnuts   Filberts

English, Roquefort and Gruyere Cheese

Crackers   Tea   Coffee

Meals, Lunches, Desserts or Fruits taken or sent to rooms, and all dishes ordered not on Bill of Fare will be Charged Extra.

The Sunday dinner menu for the WEST END HOTEL, July 26, 1903.

COURTESY OF PHIL DELCAMP

As times changed, so did the menu. Rather simple by 1903, it no longer was the epicurean's delight of days gone by. In these later years, the crowds at Long Branch were not the same as they were two decades earlier. Business declined and the WEST END HOTEL closed its doors in 1904. The building was then demolished and in 1906 it was replaced by a new structure, the TAKANASSEE HOTEL.

A photograph by G. W. Pach of an architect's drawing of the HOWLAND HOTEL
(ca. 1866) .

A quiet moment in the day at the HOWLAND HOTEL
as a northwest breeze brings a cooling effect to the shore.

PACH STEREOGRAPH # 127A, CA. 1872

The Howland Hotel

On Ocean Avenue, just north of the WEST END HOTEL, the HOWLAND HOUSE/HOTEL served the public for seventy-nine years. One of the very few descriptions of the hotel's early history was provided in 1868 by journalist and author of many Long Branch publications, J. H. Schenck.

> In 1827 "Obadiah Sayrs erected the older portion of this building upon twenty acres which joined (on the south) the grounds of the present STETSON HOUSE, as the SAYRS HOUSE."

(Note: In early references this structure has been called SAYRS, SAIRS and SEARS. Pronunciation played a part in that!)

> "It contained some sixty rooms. Eleven years afterward Sayrs sold to George Robbins, who kept the house four seasons, when it was bought by Mr. Barclay, who disposed of it at once to Mr. Henry Howland. He enlarged and remodelled it at various intervals, and during this term of twenty-four years has actively managed the hotel. For five years Messrs. Jacob Herbert and B. C. White were associated with him.

> The present capacity is designed for about three hundred guests. The rates charged are about the same as other first class houses, and the success of its management is best attested by the fact that some of the best families of the Quaker City have continued to summer under its roof for about a quarter of a century! Indeed, there are some of these who were original guests at the opening, *forty years* since! and from this period down to that of a score of years, may be named the most substantial Philadelphians, such as the families of Biddle, Fisher, Evans, Kuhn, Leaming, Markoe, Wharton, Peppers, Scott, Servis, Carnac, Williams, &.,&., embracing a large class of retired business men, imparting a certain degree of exclusiveness to the guests, devoid, however, of objectionable concomitants."[1]

Almost every successful hotel that existed over a number of years was often remodeled and expanded. This structure was no exception. By 1868 the HOWLAND HOTEL, as noted earlier, had the capacity at that time to provide accommodations for 300 guests.

57

From 1874 there is a more detailed description that mentions the further increased capacity and some of the improvements and "modern" conveniences now found in this long respected hotel.

"The HOWLAND HOUSE", with a frontage of 322 feet, is considered the handsomest hotel on the Beach. It is a quiet place, and patronized by a very superior class of guests, many of whom have been annual guests for a long series of years. That glum, irresponsible species, known as "transient," do not take up all the best rooms. And somehow it happens that no one ever registers at the "Howland" once with out bringing up there again to stop a longer while, and sure to bring his family with him.

The house can provide for 480 people, and the prices, during July and August, are $ 4.50 per day, with a reduction to permanent guests. Mr. H. Howland and his son, Mr. H. W. Howland, are the proprietors. Among the features of this house are the bath-rooms and water-closets on every floor, and Chester's Electric Annunciator - the best in use - which affords communication between the hotel office and every room in the house.

Croquet grounds in the front and rear lawns invite the pretty belles and the gallant beaux to try their skill with the mallet and the ball. There is a very fine, social, homelike feeling, which seems to pertain to this hotel, and morning concerts and evening hops are among the pleasant features.

The table is supplied direct from the Howland gardens and the Howland farm, the latter some four miles away. The "Bather" for this house, Mr. James Wooley, has been connected with it in that capacity for sixteen years. He has about forty bath-houses.

Visitors to the Branch will find a curiosity in the office of this hotel. It is a painting of the primitive hotel at the Branch - The OLD HOWLAND HOUSE - sacredly preserved by Mr. Howland, Senior, who has something to be proud of in having managed in a successful and acceptable manner a hostelry here for more than thirty-five years."[2]

Mr. Howland and other individuals continued to operate the hotel until 1875. That company then sold the business to R.J. Dobbins. At that time Boothby and Mulford assumed management of the hotel.

HOWLAND HOTEL,
Long Branch.

BOOTHBY & MULFORD, -   Managers.

Will maintain its high reputation for first-class

appointments in every department,

for the season of

1878.

A new and elegant Dining Hall has just

been added, with high arched ceiling.

Broad lawns extending to the ocean.

Only green terraced sea wall on the Branch.

Hot and Cold Salt Water Baths at hand.

Excellent Stabling.

Moderate terms to families and season guests.

A new advertisement appeared in 1878 noting a "new and elegant Dining Hall had just been added, with high arched ceilings."
BRIGHTONS OF AMERICA, 1878

Accompanying the above advertisement were these comments:

"When, in '75 Mr. R. J. Dobbins became the purchaser, Messrs. Boothby & Mulford assumed the management. Mr. P. S. Boothby was remarkably successful with the U. S. Hotel at Philadelphia, during the Centennial, and under his efficient management the Howland ranks second to none for comfort and excellent cuisine. Among this year's improvements is a new and elegant dining hall."[3]

In reviewing the written accounts of the Grand Hotels from 1860 through 1880, it is apparent that two items were quite important to the proprietors of these hotels. The reputation of all of these hotels depended a great deal on the quality of the cuisine offered to their patrons. Good food –

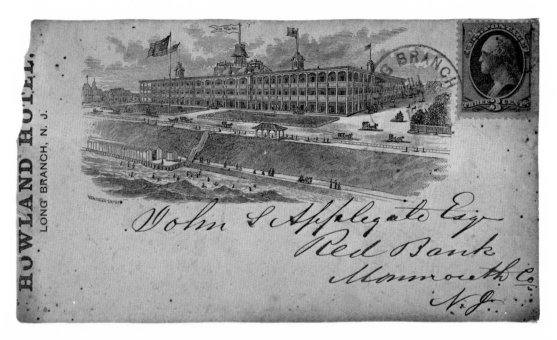

A delightful advertising cover offers an overall view of the HOWLAND HOTEL *and grounds and their relationship to the bluff, beach and ocean.*

JULY 29, 1878

pleased patrons. From the largest to the smallest hotels, for entertainment of their guests, the quality of the orchestras and the frequent dances, the fashionable Hops, were equally important. These were significant social events.

> "The Complimentary Hop given by the proprietors of this hotel, on Wednesday evening was eminently successful, and the efforts of the proprietors to make it a first-class ball, were fully sustained. At an early hour the large dancing room was a wilderness of life and gayety; the dress and adornments of the ladies who thronged within its walls, were rich, varied and truly beautiful. The music was furnished by the 7th Regiment Band, of New York City, and the ball was kept up with spirit until a late hour. The supper room was in charge of a competent caterer, and all the delicacies that the

season affords were served up in handsome style."

The last Grand Hop at the CONTINENTAL, a hotel that had four times the capacity of the Howland, was held the following Friday evening and was reported in the same article as above.

> "When the reader takes into consideration the mammoth proportions of the CONTINENTAL dining hall, and then imagine it filled with sets of dancers, all moving as if by magic to the charmed music of Faeber's best efforts, he can form some idea of the scene of Friday night. Costly dresses, flashing jewelry and diamonds, the little bits of gossip indulged in by confidential parties at intervals in the dance, little flirtations, quite unintentional; all these and many more sights, scenes and observations are the regular attendants of a grand ball..."[4]

This advertisement, published in PUCK MAGAZINE *in 1889, was typical of the period.*

Possibly a Fourth of July photograph of these guests of the HOWLAND HOTEL.
PACH PHOTOGRAPH, 1902

By 1888, the capacity of the HOWLAND HOTEL was further expanded to accommodate over 500 guests. The following year Henry Walter became the new proprietor of the Hotel.

The end, however, finally came to this once popular and "handsomest" of hotels as a result of a winter storm that damaged the building beyond repair. Eventually the structure was torn down and, in September of 1906, in a not uncommon event, the entire contents of the hotel were offered for sale.

Best Opportunity!
Greatest Bargains!

EVER OFFERED IN

LONG = BRANCH

EVERYTHING CONTAINED IN THE

HOWLAND HOTEL

will be sold at prices far below their value. No reasonable offer refused. Every fair price accepted.

Don't delay inspecting the goods. The sooner you call the better selection you can make.

D. ELINSKY

An advertisement from the LONG BRANCH DAILY RECORD, *September 17, 1906.*

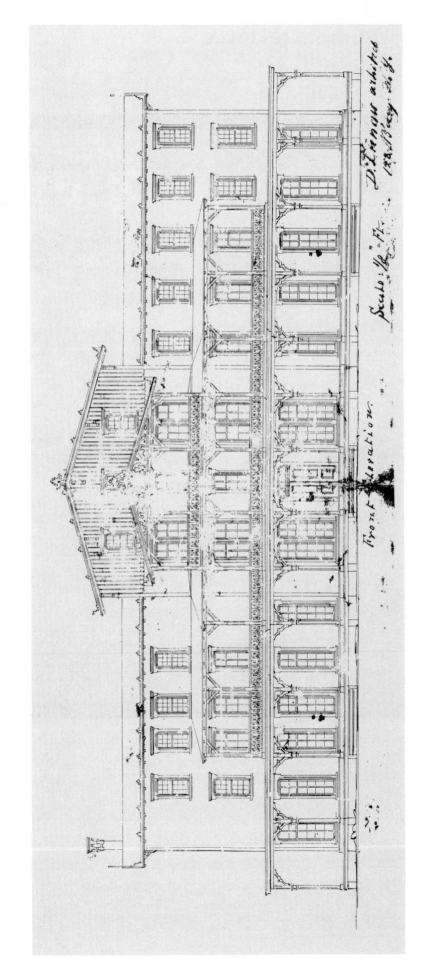

The New York architect D. Lienau's original 1868 blueprint of IAUCH'S HOTEL illustrates the front view of the new structure.

Anthony Iauch's Hotel. More than twenty adults and children posed happily on the balconies and grounds for this photographic moment.

PACH STEREOGRAPH #128, CA. 1872

Iauch's Hotel – Hotel Pannaci

On Ocean Avenue near North Bath Avenue, the site of IAUCH'S HOTEL was little more than four blocks north of the HOWLAND HOUSE.

In *ENTERTAINING A NATION*, (1940) there is a reference to a hotel "founded in 1852" called McCormick's which "was taken over some time between 1868 and 1870 by A. Iauch and renamed for him."[1]

To date, the name McCormick has not appeared in any existing archival hotel records. The name "Mrs. McCormick" does appear on a Beers map of 1860. It is, however, located north of the property that later became Iauch's and is not identified in any way as a hotel or even a very small boarding house.

According to existing documents, Anthony Iauch, of New York City, purchased property from Aaron Jacobs early in 1868. A three and a half story building was then erected and became IAUCH'S HOTEL. At the same time a small cottage called "Brignoli" was also built nearby for Mr. Iauch and his wife.

The following June, this advertisement appeared in a New York newspaper:

"IAUCH'S HOTEL, Long Branch, Shore road, now open for the reception of guests. Particular attention is called to the Restaurant, the most elegant at this fashionable Summer resort, and to the Confectionery connected with the hotel, in which the choicest dishes and his renowned ice-cream will be served at all hours; several splendid parlors reserved for private dinners and parties."[2]

This notice appeared in the *LONG BRANCH NEWS* in early July:

"A. IAUCH'S HOTEL, RESTAURANT, AND CONFECTIONERY Ocean Avenue, Long Branch. No pains have been spared by its well known proprietor to give THIS ESTABLISHMENT all the comfort and RECHERCHE that can be desired by the most select society. A well appointed Restaurant and Confectionery are connected with the hotel, and the most delicate fancy dishes and ICE CREAMS will be served at all hours. Several splendidly fitted-up saloons are reserved for private dinners, parties, etc."[3]

By mid August of 1869, the French Refectory (dining hall) at this new establishment was acknowledged a success almost from the day it opened. A superb cuisine was the main attraction of the new hotel. It was stated "IAUCH'S HOTEL became the exceedingly smart place for distinguished foreigners, diplomats and fashionable adventurers."

Anthony Iauch ran his establishment in much the same fashion as the most popular hotels at the Branch. It was observed, for example, that

> "The Hop at Iauch's Hotel Saturday evening (August 13, 1869), was a very pleasant and enjoyable affair. Mr. Iauch understands the art of hotel keeping thoroughly, and especially the management of Hops, and with his genial, gentlemanly manner it would bring him a host of guests, not counting the attractions of his house."[4]

Prior to coming to Long Branch, Mr. Iauch was well known as a "French Confectioner" (one who made or sold candy, ice cream and sweets) at his New York location at 864 Broadway on the corner of 17th Street and Union Square.

For a number of years Anthony Iauch continued to enjoy his reputation as a superior "French Confectioner" at both his older and well-known New York establishment at 864 Broadway and his new

endeavor at the Jersey Shore. His hotel in Long Branch was particularly well-known for the quality of its "Restaurant and Confectionery" as well as the ability to supply excellent "Parties and Dinners."

In 1877, a weekly column appeared in another New York newspaper describing the beginning of the summer season at Long Branch and the status of the various local hotels.

> ..."IAUCH'S HOTEL and restaurant, which are already open, also show evidence of improvement. The hotel contains about 100 rooms. The restaurant is very well known, being regarded the Delmonico's of the Branch and is greatly frequented by wealthy Germans and other foreigners, as well as by no small numbers of natives."[5]

According to the 1888 Edition of *APPLETON'S GENERAL GUIDE TO THE UNITED STATES AND CANADA*, it was one of the good hotels on a smaller scale which also included the well-known UNITED STATES HOTEL.

In 1899 the hotel was purchased by another New Yorker, Gernando Pannaci, who renamed it

Patrons of IAUCH'S HOTEL are about to depart for a morning drive.
A foreign visitor kept this stereograph as a treasured souvenir. On the reverse, written in Spanish,
was the notation "Long Branch and my surroundings. Estados Unidos."
PACH STEREOGRAPH #128B, CA. 1872

*This, the earliest known illustration of the H*OTEL
P*ANNACI, shows the new addition of the fourth floor and
the enlarged balconies. The renovated restaurant was
also featured for the first time.*

POSTCARD, CA. 1902

*A later illustration shows the first phase in "modernizing" the exterior of the H*OTEL
P*ANNACI. The balconies have been redesigned while the piazza is partially enclosed.*

POSTCARD, CA. 1908

the HOTEL PANNACI. He also enlarged the hotel by adding a fourth floor, extended the balconies and featured the Restaurant.

Mr. Pannaci, who was fluent in French, Italian, Spanish and English, had an impressive background in managing various prestigious restaurants, clubs and hotels in New York. For two years, he was also the respected proprietor and lessee of the PLIMPTON HOUSE on Watch Hill, Rhode Island, before coming to the Jersey Shore.

As soon as IAUCH'S HOTEL became the HOTEL PANNACI, there was one major change to be made. Of prime importance was that the hotel be properly identified. The name Pannaci had to appear on all the previously owned hotel silverware as soon as possible. This was typical when hotels changed names. (There is evidence that the STETSON HOUSE went through the same situation when it became the WEST END HOTEL.) As a result Iauch's

name, where possible, was removed and replaced by Pannaci's.

In the busy and successful years that followed in Long Branch, the HOTEL PANNACI was twice modernized and enlarged to accommodate 250 guests. In 1907, it was reported in a local paper:

> "The HOTEL PANNACI has been completely modernized and refurnished. The furniture is in harmony with the decorations. Old-time guests of the hotel hardly recognized the interiors so thorough has been the change."[6]

By 1910, one of the major changes was the installation of steam heat to make it an up-to-date winter hotel. Other plans included building an addition to the south end of the structure and glass enclosing the entire piazza. The dining room was also doubled in size to seat 150 patrons. Continuing in the tradition of Anthony Iauch, the Hotel Pannaci was noted for its "celebrated cuisine in both its Restaurant and Cafe." That continuing reputation for excellent food was a major attraction that brought visitors back year after year.

Mr. Pannaci became a Director of the local Board of Trade in 1906 and helped organize the Long Branch Hotel Men's Association. After Mr. Pannaci died in 1923, his wife managed the hotel until operations ceased in 1932. The building was demolished that year after being part of the hotel history of Long Branch since 1868.

Gernando Pannaci's brother, Eduardo, also from New York, had the same background and experience in the restaurant and hotel business. He became the owner and successful operator of his own HOTEL PANNACI in nearby Sea Bright from 1887 until he died in 1944. The hotel, closed for a few years, was eventually sold and reopened as the CHARLES MANOR. Unfortunately, the building became the victim of a spectacular fire on Halloween Eve in 1953 and burned to the ground.

Menu

PONCIRES

ESSENCE DE VOLAILLE EN TASSE

AMANDES SALEES

CELERI   OLIVES   RADIS

OEUFS COCOTTE

COEUR DE FILET DE BOEUF, CHEZ SOIS

PIGEONNEAUX GRILLES

SALADE DE LAITUE

GLACES

PETITS FOURS

BONBONS

CAFE

HAUTE SAUTERNE   RUINART BRUT

POLAND WATER   APOLLINARIS

HOTEL PANNACI
OCEAN AVENUE
LONG BRANCH, N. J.   SEPTEMBER 28TH, 1908

An example of a wedding luncheon menu from the HOTEL PANNACI.
SEPTEMBER 28, 1908

On coffee pots, creamers, pitchers and similar large items, the name IAUCH is found stamped underneath the base. This example (ca. 1869) is from a small coffee pot made by the Manhattan Plate Co. of New York.

In 1899, when IAUCH's HOTEL became the PANNACI HOTEL, all the existing silverware underwent a name change. The name Pannaci, for example, was engraved on the side of this same coffee pot.

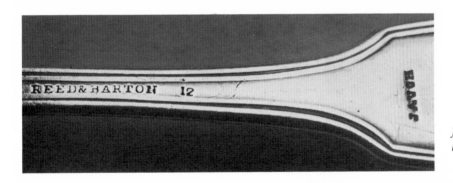

Iauch's name, in very small letters is found on the under side of the spoons and forks. This example is on a spoon made by Reed and Barton.

Mr. Pannaci was fortunate that he was able to have his name easily engraved on the appropriate place on most of the silverware. This example is an oyster fork with his newly applied name.

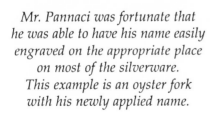

This photo-postcard shows the final changes in the architecture of the HOTEL PANNACI. The piazza is fully enclosed while the addition to the rear of the hotel's south side is also completed.

POSTCARD, 1910

As the twentieth century arrived, so did the newest innovation – the automobile. By 1913, more and more excited visitors were now coming to the Shore by automobile. This new development was recognized in many different ways.

A 1913 advertisement stated the HOTEL PANNACI was an Officially Appointed Hotel of The Automobile Club of America.

H. Woodleaf and family,	New York
Marquis of St. Mazzano and family,	Turin, Italy
F. C. Hollins and family,	New York
P. McElroy and family,	New York
M. Herzog and family,	New York
Annsberger and family,	New York
Mrs. Frankenheimer and daughters,	New York
A. Casanova and family,	Havana
W. C. Dickels,	New York
A. C. Fransioli and family,	Brooklyn
E. P. Osborn,	New York
F. W. Muser and family,	New York

A partial list of visitors staying at IAUCH'S HOTEL *in 1874.*

HOTEL PANNACI
MRS. GERNANDO PANNACI
Owner and Proprietor
LONG BRANCH, N. J.

An example of an envelope used by the HOTEL PANNACI *during the hotel's last years.*

CA. 1930

FRANK LESLIE'S ILLUSTRATED NEWSPAPER

Entered according to Act of Congress, in the year 1857, by FRANK LESLIE, in the Clerk's Office of the District Court for the Southern District of New York. (Copyrighted June 14, 1858.)

No. 133—VOL VI.]   NEW YORK, SATURDAY, JUNE 19, 1858.   [PRICE 6 CENTS.

CONTENTS.

SUMMER WATERING-PLACES.
No. 1.—Long Branch.

SUMMER is come upon us with a vigor that opens every pore and starts the eager perspiration with a copious flow, to the manifest destruction of spotless shirt fronts and stand-up collars, and to the excessive annoyance of fat-faced men. There rises up one universal cry for ice, and fluids are dashed down thirsty throats without regard to the quantity which, according to the best medical authorities, one is supposed to hold. There is a heavy run upon the Croton, and it is said by those who mix with the great world, that other fluids with various names are sometimes mingled with the pure Croton; but for this statement we will not vouch. Enough to say that summer has come, that "leafy June" marched in upon us with blazing colors, that it is hot, very hot, remarkably hot, and that bipeds and quadrupeds are alike panting for a cool breeze and for a cool place wherein to enjoy it. Now is the time for strawberries (without milk or cream, in these swill times), and peas, and other luscious fruits and vegetables.

Now is the time when the denizens of our crowded cities begin to realize the fact, that there is pure, fresh, invigorating air somewhere about. They now begin to think of the far-off mountains, the quiet farm-yards, with the pastoral cows swinging their unshorn tails, and drink, in imagination, deep draughts of the rich and health-giving milk; visions of sea-side retreats, with bracing air, delicious bathing, and the glorious, ever-changing ocean, with its impressive grandeur, are ever before them, and the spirit of unrest seizes hold of them, and papa or husband knows no rest until the health of the family is consulted, and a trip to the country or to the coast duly organized and carried out. Happy are they whose means enable them to seek the pure air, and draw a new existence from this the surest of all restoratives.

The pleasantest of all our near-by watering-places is Long Branch. It is situated upon our magnificent bay, a short distance up the Shrewsbury river, and a little over two hours' sail from the city. Formerly the boats could not approach Long Branch within several miles, and a long and hot ride across the sands was the consequence; but now the passengers are landed close by the hotels, which is certainly a great improvement.

There are ten or a dozen hotels at Long Branch, of which the United States Hotel, which is represented in our drawing, is among the best conducted and most commodious of the first-class hotels in the country. The hotels all stand along the brow of a plateau, which extends a mile or two along the coast at a height of about fifty feet above the sea. The houses stand back some two hundred feet from the edge of the plateau, so that a broad and unbroken terrace for promenading purposes is presented nearly the whole length of the elevation. There are many beautiful villas about, and the hotels are surrounded by charming lawns, so that the place presents the pleasures of the country retreat and the seaside sociability. It is a pleasant sight to see the broad promenade in front of the hotels crowded with beautiful ladies, and the accompanying sterner sex; and to see how the children revel in the cool evening breezes that come over the sea for the special delectation of the Long Branch residents.

The United States Hotel, kept by Mr. Crater, is, as we have said, a commodious first-class hotel. It is conducted upon a most liberal scale, and the charges are moderate; the attendance is capital, and the host, by his attention to the comforts of his guests and his urbane and pleasant manner, is very popular with all who throng his hotel every year. The bathing is of course one of the principal features of a residence at Long Branch. To this Mr. Crater pays particular care. Flags are used as signals for the bathing times of the ladies, gentlemen and children, and an expert swimmer is stationed outside the bathers, so that children and others can enjoy the delicious bath without any fear of unfortunate consequences. Ropes and other safeguards are also plentifully distributed. There are fine stables at the United States Hotel, and what with the beautiful rides around the adjacent country, and the fine row and sail boats on the river, and the numerous hops given several times in each week by Mr. Crater, if life does not pass pleasantly at Long Branch it will not be because the proprietor of the United States Hotel has neglected any means of furthering that desirable end. We have passed many pleasant summer weeks at Long Branch, and we should be glad to have our friends share in our happy experience.

SUMMER WATERING-PLACES LONG BRANCH VIEW OF THE UNITED STATES HOTEL.

This early wood engraving of the UNITED STATES HOTEL shows the building many years before a fourth floor was added and the design of the roof changed.

Here is the remodeled and enlarged UNITED STATES HOTEL. It appears that some of the original building (with three floors) was still retained at the southern end of the Hotel (left side of photo). The rest of the structure was enlarged to four floors.

PACH STEREOGRAPH #81A, CA. 1870

The United States Hotel

It often was an adventure to travel from New York City to Long Branch. A typical boat trip from the City to the Branch was documented by a summer visitor in a *FRANK LESLIE'S ILLUSTRATED NEWSPAPER* article in 1857. It certainly was an interesting and picturesque way to arrive at a hotel on the Jersey Shore. The visitor wrote...

> ..."safely embarked on board the enterprising little steamer *Alice Price*, at the foot of Robinson street, it was but a short time before we were clear of the forests of shipping which fill the New York Harbor, and en route for Long Branch. Three boats leave daily for this watering-place, one generally starting in the morning and two in the afternoon, but the exact hour of their departure is for the most part regulated by the tides."

Crossing the Lower Bay to Sandy Hook, the *Alice Price* entered the Shrewsbury River. Shortly after passing the Highlands of Nevesink the steamer landed its passengers at the OCEAN HOUSE dock. This small hotel was located on the river side of the northern portion of the barrier beach that later became Sea Bright. (The fare for the two

hour trip from New York was only twenty-five cents).

This obscure, but important reference to Anthony Haggerty's OCEAN HOUSE, was published in the *NEW YORK TRIBUNE* almost a decade earlier in the summer of 1848:

> "The steamboat ORUS makes a daily trip to and from Red Bank, Shrewsbury Inlet, N.J. stopping at the little known OCEAN HOUSE and landing passengers for Long Branch. It is remarkable that the advantages of this sea-side resort are better known to and appreciated by Philadelphians than New-Yorkers, though it is less than three hours sail from us and three times as far from Philadelphia, to say nothing of the counter attraction of Cape May. Monmouth County looks her best at present, and is visibly increasing in wealth, industry and production."[1]

Continuing our traveller's previous story of 1857, on landing at the OCEAN HOUSE, he noted that fellow passengers

> "...found a number of "beach carriages," as they are called, awaiting the arrival of the boat

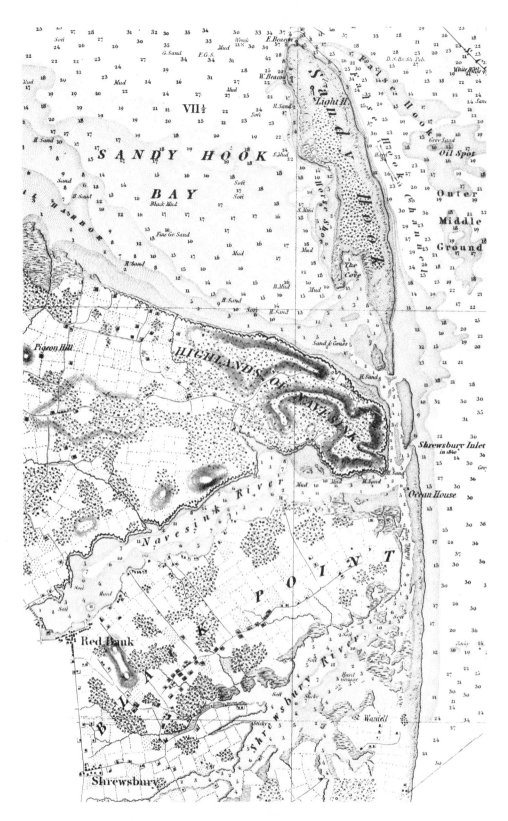

An excerpt from a "Map of New-York Bay and Harbor and the Environs" from a Survey of the Coast of the United States published by the Coast Survey Department, Washington, D.C., 1845. This shows Sandy Hook as an island and the Shrewsbury Inlet (the "inside run" from the Atlantic Ocean to the Navesink River). The OCEAN HOUSE can be seen located in what is now Sea Bright.

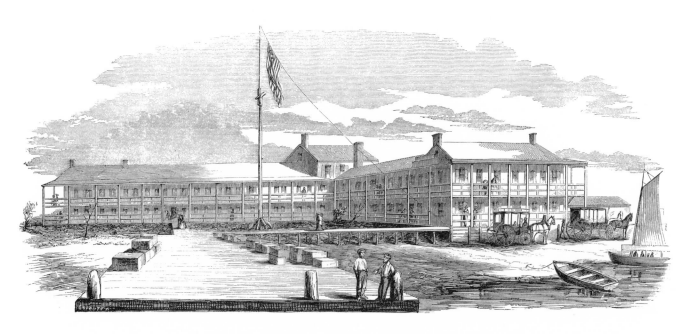

This view from the Shrewsbury River of Haggerty's OCEAN HOUSE and dock illustrates the landing place for New York boats that brought visitors on their way to the Long Branch hotels.

FRANK LESLIE'S ILLUSTRATED NEWSPAPER, AUGUST 22, 1857

These wide-wheeled carriages continued south along the barrier beach slowly conveying the newly-arrived visitors to their final destination - Long Branch.

FRANK LESLIE'S ILLUSTRATED NEWSPAPER, AUGUST 22, 1857

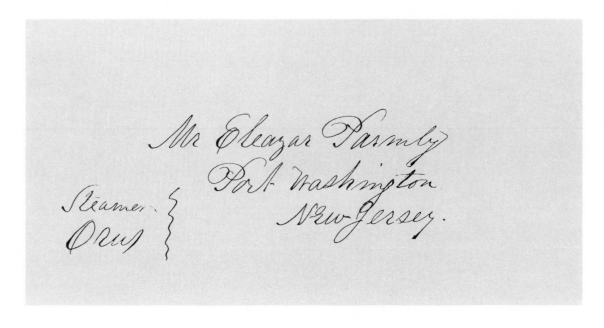

FOR SHREWSBURY,
Port Washington, Brown's Dock, Middletown, and
Red Bank.
THE STEAMER
O R U S,
CAPTAIN C. PRICE,
Will run as follows, from Fulton Market Slip.

LEAVES N. YORK		SHREWSBURY.	
December.		December.	
Tuesday, 1	at 1 P.M.	Wednesday 2	2 P.M
Thursday, 3	2 1-2	Friday 4	9
Saturday, 5	9 A.M	Monday 7	10
Tuesday 8	10	Wednesday 9	10
Thursday 10	10	Friday 11	11
Saturday 12	12 M.	Monday 14	12 M.
Tuesday 15	12	Wednesday 16	1 P M
Thursday 17	1 P.M	Friday 18	2
Saturday 19	2 1-2	Monday 21	10 A.M
Tuesday 22	9 1 2 AM	Wednesday 23	10
Thursday 24	10	Friday 25	11
Saturday 26	12 M.	Monday 28	1 P.M.
Tuesday 29	1 P.M	Weds'day 30	1
Thursday 31	1		

An 1846 schedule for the Steamer Orus.

from New York, to take its passengers to Long Branch. They are curious looking but but very convenient vehicles, with broad wheels, formed so as to travel with greater ease along the yielding sands."

This desolate stretch of sand was, nevertheless, a long slow ride which would ultimately bring the

passengers to their final destination — the UNITED STATES HOTEL, at Ocean Avenue just south of Chelsea Avenue. At this point our newly arrived and tired visitor went directly to his room. He continued his narrative stating his accommodations were:

"...a cheerful little apartment which had the advantage of being quiet and secluded, even in the whirl and bustle of a large and populous hotel like this, to get rid of the dust and heat of travel, and after having "renovated" our selves, we again descended to the animated scene below.

Here, by the way, let us say a word about the *table d'hote* of the UNITED STATES HOTEL. At the generality of watering places the fare is decidedly indifferent; people seem to take it for granted that you have left all gastronomic tastes and preferences behind you, in New York, or Philadelphia, or wherever your hailing place may happen to be. But here everything is in the most perfect style, and on inquiry the fact was accounted for at once. Most of the cooks and stewards are from the ST. NICHOLAS HOTEL, and take great pride in the proper administration of their respective departments.

Everything about the UNITED STATES HOTEL is perfect. It is a first-class hotel, and has ample accommodations for at least three hundred guests. Wide and roomy piazzas enclose the building on three sides, and afford charming

A letter carried by the Steamer Orus to Port Washington (now Rumson).
SEPTEMBER 4, 1846

lounges for those who like to enjoys a picture of the sea in three different directions, and each apartment has access to this verandah by a door and window. J.A.S. Crater, the polite and gentlemanly proprietor, uses every endeavor to promote the comfort and and enjoyment of all who are under his roof...

We took a peep into the ball-room, where a brilliant hop was going on as we went by. There is a ball three times a week at the UNITED STATES, as well as the other hotels, and all outsiders, distinguished guests, and stars from other firmaments, are expected to grace the scene with their presents.

Truly it is a sight to drive any hard-hearted old bachelor nearly distracted. Just think of a room full of lovely young damsels, radiant in diamonds, roses, bright eyes and destructively piquant figures: think of the charming widows, and dashing belles, and bewitching young matrons, who carry a whole armory of Cupid's arrows in every turn of their roguish heads! Dangerous ground this, but like all other dangerous things,excessively tempting!"[2]

These, indeed, must have been the "good old days!"

In most of the "Grand Hotels" entertainment for their guests was paramount. Visitors were often able to enjoy the popular music of the period from morning through the late evening. This amenity was frequently provided by the hotel's own orchestra of choice.

The UNITED STATES HOTEL was acknowledged as a first class establishment for more than three decades. It offered a variety of events to please its clientele – even on special occasions in midwinter! A few other hotels did offer their services for winter events.

The hotel, for example, held a "Second Annual Military and Civic Ball" on the evening of February 22, 1858 on behalf of the "Second Regiment, Monmouth Brigade, given by the Ocean Rifle Guard, Company B." A hand written note on the back of one invitation advised - "If the Evening should prove Stormy the Ball will be Adjourned until the next fair one."

A further newspaper article describing the UNITED STATES HOTEL appeared later during the summer of the same year. It read in part:

This is an early example of a hotel advertising cover printed for the UNITED STATES HOTEL by Neville of New York.

LONG BRANCH, JULY 21, 1857

"There are ten or a dozen hotels at Long Branch (not all on Ocean Avenue), of which the UNITED STATES HOTEL...is among the best conducted and most commodious of the first-class hotels in the country. (Most) of the hotels stand along the brow of a plateau, which extends a mile or two along the coast at a height of about fifty feet above the sea. The house stands back some two hundred feet from the edge of the plateau, so that a broad and unbroken terrace for promenading purposes is presented nearly the whole length of the elevation. There are many beautiful villas about, and the hotels are surrounded by charming lawns, so that the place presents the pleasures of the country retreat and the seaside sociability. It is a pleasant sight to see the broad promenade in front of the hotels crowded with beautiful ladies, and the accompanying sterner sex; and to see how the children revel in the cool evening breezes that come over the sea for the special delectation of the Long Branch residents.

The UNITED STATES HOTEL, kept by Mr. Crater, is, as we have said, a commodious first-class hotel. It is conducted upon a most liberal scale, and the charges are moderate; the attendance is capital, and the host, by his attention to the comforts of his guests and his urbane and pleasant manner, is very popular with all who throng to his hotel every year. The bathing is of course one of the principal features of a residence at Long Branch. To this Mr. Crater pays particular care. Flags are used as signals for the bathing times of the ladies, gentlemen and children, and an expert swimmer is stationed outside the bathers, so that the children and others can enjoy the delicious bath without any fear of unfortunate consequences. ropes and other safeguards are also plentifully distributed. There are fine stables at the UNITED STATES HOTEL, and what with the beautiful rides around the adjacent country, and the fine row and sail boats on the river, and the numerous hops given several times each week by Mr. Crater, if life does not pass pleasantly at Long Branch it will not be because the proprietor of the UNITED STATES HOTEL has neglected any means of furthering that desirable end. We have passed many pleasant summer weeks at Long Branch, and we should be glad to have our friends share in our happy experience."[3]

A decade later, in 1868, additional comments offered still another word picture of this favored establishment.

"..the UNITED STATES HOTEL, built in 1852, by F. Kennedy, Messrs. George and Isaac Crater being associated with him. In 1855 it was bought by Benjamin Shoemaker and W. Stokes. The latter gentlemen, however, withdrew, and Mr. Shoemaker conducted it until his death, in 1866, when it was leased for the season to Chas. Pitman, who ran it for that year as the PITMAN HOUSE.

Being subsequently disposed of at administrator's sale, it passed into the hands of Mr. Samuel Laird in 1868. He at once thoroughly renovated and improved the surroundings and newly furnished it in every part with carpets and furniture of excellent quality. The character of the house passed through a transforming process, and it is thoroughly a first-

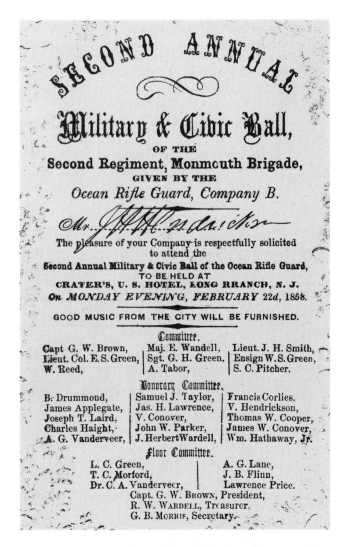

The invitation to the Second Annual Military & Civic Ball held at Crater's UNITED STATES HOTEL, at Long Branch, on the evening of February 22, 1858. "Weather permitting" was noted on the back.

*The "finest croquet lawns" and the music were
attractions that brought many visitors to the Hotel.*
BRIGHTONS OF AMERICA. 1878

class hotel. The capacity of the house is for
about three hundred guests. Mr. Laird conducts
it in connection with the MANSION HOUSE, and
imparts the same genial esprit under his peculiar regime.

There are thirteen acres of ground in connection with the premises, neatly laid out for
hotel purposes."[4]

A few years later, Laird and Van Cleaf became
the sole proprietors. The "finest croquet lawns"
and the music were attractions that brought many
visitors to this hotel.

In 1874, DEARBORN'S GUIDEBOOK provided yet
another glimpse into what a visitor could expect
at the UNITED STATES HOTEL:

"M. M. Laird, proprietor, Charles B. Potter
and J. C. Van Cleaf, the polite and gentlemanly
clerks, will leave no effort untried, to secure for
the guests of this house all the comforts that
can be found at any first-class hotel in the land.
The States has been re-painted throughout, and
very extensively re-furnished for the present
season; it fronts the ocean, and has a grand lawn
for croquet parties, and others who like to gam-
bol on the green. The band, under the leadership of Carl Sohst, will discourse sweet strains,
morning and evening during the season. Mr.
Laird's long experience in ministering to the
wants of the public as a hotel-keeper, is a sufficient assurance that he knows how to keep a
hotel, and will do it.

Terms for July and August, $4 per day, or
$25 per week.

During June and September, $21 per week."[5]

In 1902, near the end of its days, Joseph M.
Downing was the proprietor of the UNITED STATES
HOTEL.

In the distance, on Ocean Avenue, one can see the MANSION HOUSE at the extreme left (obscured a bit by the Sea Side Chapel), the CENTRAL HOTEL (center) and the UNITED STATES HOTEL on the extreme right. West of, or in back of, fashionable Ocean Avenue, Long Branch was still quite rural.

PACH STEREOGRAPH #52, CA. 1874

This view of the CENTRAL HOTEL also captures the image of the "Fruit Depot" just south of the main building as well as the hotel's Bar (which has a "Lager Bier" sign in the window. The CENTRAL HOTEL was under the management of Vollmer and Jauss at this time.

PACH STEREOGRAPH #100B, CA. 1875

One of the two known stereographic views of the newly-built CENTRAL HOTEL.
At this time it was under the proprietorship of H.C. Shoemaker.
PACH STEREOGRAPH #100A, CA. 1873

The Central Hotel

Opened for the first time in June of 1873, the short-lived and little-known CENTRAL HOTEL was located on Ocean Avenue just south of the MANSION HOUSE.

One of the first local advertisements declared the hotel

> "...will be open for the reception of guests JUNE 5th, and continue open during the entire year.The CENTRAL is a NEW HOTEL, having never before been occupied. It Has Sixty-three First-Class Bed Rooms, all newly and completely furnished with bell from each room to the office; a large portion of the rooms being furnished with grates and fire-places for Fall and Winter occupation.
>
> The hotel is the best located of any on the shore, commanding from its balconies a View of the Drive the Entire Length of the Beach, which no other hotel gives. It has a neat Lawn in front, well guarded for the protection of children. The Bluff has been sloped down to the top of a breakwater five feet high, furnishing easy access to the best Bathing afforded by any hotel on the beach, the bathing ground being in full view from the hotel balconies.
>
> Its location: its large and well furnished rooms; its pleasant and well lighted parlors, make it one of the most attractive and comfortable hotels along the beach.
>
> We shall endeavor to conduct the Culinary department so as to render this hotel second to none in the country. For terms of Board and other particulars, address H. C. Shoemaker, Proprietor."[1]

A similar but more revealing description of the hotel appeared early in the following season of 1874:

> "The CENTRAL HOTEL is aptly named, for it is the most central, and in many respects the best located hotel on the Beach. It is the only hotel from whose balconies a full view of the bathing ground, the entire length of the beach, and of Ocean avenue can be obtained.
>
> It is comparatively a new building, having been built but one year. It is a tasteful, ornamental structure, with the latest improvements, and is fitted up with fire-places and grates for cool weather. Several important alterations have been made before the opening of the present season, and we can most cordially com-

mend the CENTRAL as a comfortable, well-furnished house.

We take pleasure also in commending the management of the hotel. It is kept in a most excellent manner by Mr. H. C. Shoemaker, who was formerly associated with his father in the management of the UNITED STATES HOTEL. About one hundred and twenty-five guests can be accommodated at the CENTRAL, and they will be comfortably cared for. The terms are reasonable and the table superior.

Mr. Geo. A. Shoemaker has charge of the office - (he was also formerly associated with his father, Benjamin, at the UNITED STATES HOTEL) a fact which will give great satisfaction to the old friends who may come this season, as well as to all new ones after they have found him out. The bar is well stocked with the choicest wines and liquors, and is under the care of Mr. J. F. Van Dyke, who is a quiet, genial fellow, and square as a brick, as all will find who have the good fortune to come in contact with him."[2]

At street level, within the south end of the hotel, was a bar that featured "Lager Bier." A small store adjoining the south end of the building was the "Fruit Depot."

Of the two known stereographic views of the hotel, #100b shows the bar with a "Lager Bier" sign in the window as well as bunches of bananas hanging under the awning of the "Fruit Depot" at the extreme left. Stereographic view # 100a, the northern end of the building, depicts the CENTRAL HOTEL Drugstore and Telegraph Office. For obvious, but different reasons, both the Bar and the Drugstore were often frequented and very much appreciated by many visitors of the local scene.

Furthermore:

"Abundant opportunity is afforded those who have occasion to visit emporiums of art and fashion...The flashing establishments in (nearby) Atlantic Block, as well as several others in the village, cater entirely to the fashionable visitor. Everything desireable in the way of laces, feathers, diamonds and ornaments, and elegant dress goods, are obtainable. The most popular resort of the elite is under the CENTRAL HOTEL, and is conducted by Mrs. Davis."[3]

In stereograph #100b, the sign and store of Mrs. Davis can be identified (to the right of center) in the front of the hotel. Among the "emporiums of art and fashion" found there was photographer Colwell Lane's Galleries. Lane was quite popular and produced a number of rare stereographic views of Monmouth County.

The CENTRAL HOTEL failed after one year. It was then rented by William Vollmer and Fritz Jauss in 1875 until the Hotel was ultimately destroyed by fire at the end of 1876. Ironically, in 1872, Vollmer and Jauss operated a twenty room hotel (called the EXCURSION HOUSE) and a popular Restaurant and Lager Beer Garden in Atlantic Block that was destroyed by fire in September of 1874.

This view of the "ATLANTIC BLOCK, Long Branch" captures some of the commercial spirit that attracted many hotel visitors. This particular stereographic view was produced by Colwell Lane.
NEW JERSEY STEREOSCOPIC VIEW COMPANY #88, CA. 1873
COURTESY OF KEN ROSEN

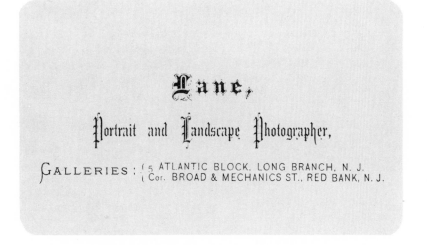

This advertisement appeared on many of Colwell Lane's photographic portraits. This example was printed on the back of a popular size called a carte-de-visite.
CA. 1873

A busy scene on Ocean Avenue in front of the Mansion House.
Fashionably dressed men, women and children socialize as they stroll and enjoy
the early morning sunshine and ocean breeze. Horse-drawn carriages and
a billy goat cart contribute to the pleasant activities of the moment.

Frank Leslie's Illustrated Newspaper, August 1, 1863

Samuel Laird's MANSION HOUSE *on Ocean Avenue and the corner of Chelsea Avenue.*

PACH STEREOGRAPH #117A, CA. 1873

The Mansion House

The MORRIS HOUSE, originally called a boarding house, was owned and operated by Jacob W. Morris. The hotel opened July 1, 1845 proudly flying one of the first United States flags to be seen on the bluff. The MORRIS HOUSE was purchased by Samuel Laird in 1852 and renamed the MANSION HOUSE. The building was then enlarged by adding a south wing and doubling the capacity. It soon developed an excellent reputation that lasted for years. President Grant stayed at both the STETSON HOUSE and the MANSION HOUSE from time to time before he moved into his cottage in Elberon in 1869.

Perhaps the most important event to take place at the MANSION HOUSE was on August 22, 1861, just four months after the Civil War erupted. On that date, Mrs. Abraham Lincoln paid a visit to Long Branch. The MANSION HOUSE was the proud hotel of choice and basked in the popularity of her arrival.

According to both the *NEW YORK HERALD* and the *NEW YORK TIMES*, Mrs. Lincoln and her entourage spent most of the first day with former Governor Newell inspecting a local Life Saving Station and witnessing a very detailed exhibition of the workings of the Life Saving Service.

In 1846, as a member of Congress, Newell first originated the Life Saving Service and saw to it that Stations were erected along the coast from Sandy Hook to Egg Harbor.

Later, in that afternoon of August of 1861, Mrs. Lincoln and excited crowds watched from the beach and the bluff in front of the MANSION HOUSE, as lifeboats were launched and a simulated rescue took place.

By sunset, Mrs. Lincoln and other guests returned to the hotel and observed a fleet of balloons rise into a turbulent sky signaling the start of the "Grand Ball" that was soon to take place. At that moment a severe rain storm drenched a planned fireworks display, much to the frustration of those in charge. In spite of the storm, the "Grand Ball" proceeded as scheduled.

Only one hundred cards were issued, admitting a gentleman and two ladies. By half past nine most guests were crowding the room. At ten o'clock, as Mrs. Lincoln and her party arrived, the band played patriotic airs and all the guests joined in a grand promenade.

"The ball was given in the dining room of the MANSION HOUSE, which was neatly and handsomely decorated with Star Spangled Banners. Dodsworth's band furnishing the music. The program of dances was as follows:

PROGRAMME DANSANT	
1. Promenade	12. Lancers
2. Quadrille	13.Schottische and Mazourka
3. Lancers	14. Quadrille
4. Polka and Redowa	15. Lancers
5. Quadrille Sociable	16. Polka and Redowa
6. Lancers	17. Quadrille
7. Polka - Danish	18. Lancers
8. Quadrille	19. Esmeralda and Polka Redowa
9. Lancers	20. Quadrille - Cheat
10. Waltz and Gallop	21.Lancers
11. Quadrille Menuet	22.Quadrille

The party was arranged in the following order for the entrance – Mrs. President Lincoln and ex-Govenor Newell, of New Jersey. Mrs Lincoln was dressed in an elegant robe of white grenadine, with a long flowing train, the bottom of the skirt puffed with quillings of white satin, and the arms and shoulder uncovered save with an elegant pointlace shawl. She wore a necklace and bracelets of superb pearls, a pearl fan, and a headdress of wreathed white wild roses. Beyond all comparison, she was the most richly and completely dressed lady present."[1]

By twelve thirty, after much dancing and supping (including platters of oysters and dishes of ice cream), Mrs. Lincoln and her party retired for the evening. The festivities continued on until 3 a.m. in the morning as the band played on.

"The "Grand Hop" in honor of Mrs. President Lincoln was a success."

The summer of 1866 also provided the guests of the MANSION HOUSE with more exciting evenings of music and dancing. The following comments provide an interesting observation of the fashions at one particular event.

"The Second Hop of the season, at the Mansion House, came off on Thursday evening, and was attended by an immense throng of the fashion and beauty of the cities, the present habitues of the Branch. The spacious dining room was cleared, and by 10 o'clock the merry dancers were whirling through the various sets of the programme.

To attempt to describe the dresses of the ladies would be a Herculean task — their richness and beauty dazzling the observer, and the bewitching music and gay scene all combined to make it an event always to be remembered with pleasure.

We caught a glimpse of a few prominent dresses as the ladies went whirling past, and made our notes thereon. It would have been more satisfactory to have given a fuller description, but under the circumstances it was not practicable:

Miss G....s, N.Y., lavender silk, corsage a la Pompadour with lace.

The belle of the evening, Miss C....r, N.J., cerise silk, hair a la Grecque, with gold bands.

Miss H....t, N.Y., pink silk, low corsage, white fringe trimmings, hair in white bands.

Miss R....t, N.Y. white tulle black lace trimming. Miss M....tt, N.Y., white tulle, hair puffed and trimmed with pearl chains.

Miss ...., N.Y., white tulle, pink peasant waist, beautiful leaf wreaths; very fine.

Mrs...., N.Y., light blue silk, low corsage, with puffed lace, skirt trimmed with white moire antique.

Miss M....r, Newark, white, blue trimming and sash.

Mrs J. T...., Trenton, brown moire antique, black lace trimmings.

Miss S....y, N.Y., green silk, black lace trimmings and shawl.

Miss D....h, N.Y., white alpaca, pink trimmings and sash, low corsage.

A lady, in delicate green silk, with long white fur trimmings, was much admired, as was one in dark blue silk, with white cords in loops and knots."[2]

This gives some idea of the "richness and beauty" that dazzled the observer and any one else who attended the Hop at the MANSION HOUSE.

Frank Leslie's Illustrated Newspaper printed an article in mid-summer of 1865 with an updated description of the Mansion House in these words:

"Among the fashionable Summer Hotels of our great Republic, the Mansion House, Long Branch, occupies a prominent position, not only on account of the spaciousness of the building, the airiness and comfort of the rooms, the healthfulness of the spot and the beauty of the location, but for that genial air of home which the proprietor, Mr. Laird, throws over it. Our engraving is so accurate, that it relieves us from the trouble of describing the exterior of the building. We shall, therefore, confine our remarks to the dining-room, which is one of the most spacious in this country.

Our readers may get some idea of its size, when we state that its dimensions are 120 feet by 80, and that it will seat over 550 persons. This model dining-room has also the unspeakable advantage of being so situated that the sun cannot reach it, a fact which can be fully appreciated in summer. It is also most admirably ventilated from the roof, with Miller's patent ventilator. All these advantages make it indisputably one of the coolest and pleasant dining-rooms in the United States. Having already borne our tribute of acknowledgement to the courteous and liberal proprietor, we trust the hostess, Mrs. Laird, will excuse us if we add that she is the greatest attraction of the house, making, by her winning and lady-like manners, her guests, more especially the fairer portion of them, feel like old friends.

Mr. Laird, like all those 'who really know how to keep a hotel,' has selected able assistants, such as Messrs. Tater and Fletcher, and Mr. Allen, the steward, one of the most judicious of providers."[3]

Besides the social affairs, a variety of indoor and outdoor sports kept the patrons entertained. While billiards and croquet were popular, baseball had quite a following. There was much competition between individual Long Branch Hotel teams. On July 23, 1866, for example, the Mansion House Base Ball Club lost a game to the Stetson House. On August 6th, however, the Mansion House walked all over the Stetson House Nine, beating them 22 to 6! Rules were different in those days. That game was called after five innings as the Stetson House gave up the contest! Eight days

"The dining room of Laird's Mansion House, Long Branch, N.J."
Frank Leslie's Illustrated Newspaper, July 15, 1865

later, the MANSION HOUSE team squeaked out a 16 to 15 victory over the "Union Base Ball Club" of neighboring Howland's Hotel. What a season!

Almost a decade later the MANSION HOUSE was still considered one of the finest hotels to be found at Long Branch. In 1874 it was stated:

"The MANSION House, Wm. L. McIntire, proprietor, is second to none at the Branch. This house, long and favorably known under the ownership of the late Samuel Laird, faces upon Ocean avenue, with a splendid lawn in front and spacious piazzas extending entirely around it. Mr. McIntire was associated with Mr. Laird for ten years in the management of the house. It has been thoroughly renovated and refurnished this season, and is better prepared than ever for the reception and comforts of its guests.

Mr. Wm. H. Burroughs, late of the St. James' Hotel, New York, and so long and favorably known in the New York and Philadelphia hotels, is the general manager, and this fact in itself is a sufficient guarantee to the public of the cordial reception and satisfactory manner with which they will be treated during their sojourn at the Mansion.

Mr. Wm. T. Burroughs, whose friends are legion, is the room clerk. Mr. A. S. Gladwin fills the office of cashier. The bar and billiard rooms of this house are in a building entirely separate from the hotel, therefore any little noise or amusement that may be going on during the height of the season, will be entirely out of the way of those that are more quietly inclined.

The billiard-room is under the charge and management of Messrs. Benjamin Whitman and Charles Dignon. Most of the tables are of the new regulation size, a fact which will be appreciated by those who understand and enjoy the game, as these are the only ones at the Branch."[4]

The hotel was did very well until it was partially destroyed by a $60,000 fire during the night of December 19, 1884. Although rebuilt by 1889, it was architecturally quite unlike the first structure. It was apparently now owned by a Mr. Mead and Mr. Turner. It was still in business in 1902 under the managment of one Nellie Maguire.

"Latest Arrivals."
LONG BRANCH NEWS, AUGUST 1866

86

MANSION HOUSE,
LONG BRANCH.

SAMUEL LAIRD, - - PROPRIETOR.

THIS sea-side "MANSION" retains its long-established popularity, and has been opened for the season of 1868, with greater improvements than ever before. The Grand Parlor is greatly enlarged, opening on three sides upon porches and lawn beyond. A large new Billiard Room is erected in rear of the Hotel, and elegantly fitted up with all the modern improvements.

The *cuisine* of the "MANSION" will be maintained in the excellence for which it has so long been celebrated.

MANSION HOUSE,
Long Branch.

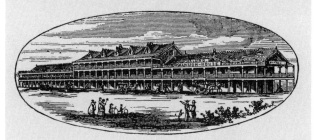

PIERIS & BUTLER, Proprietors.

This sea-side "MANSION" retains its long established popularity, and has been opened for the season of 1878 with greater improvements than ever before. A Grand Parlor has been added, opening on three sides upon porches, and lawn beyond. A new Billiard Room is erected in rear of the Hotel, and elegantly fitted up with all the modern improvements.

The *cuisine* of the "MANSION" will be maintained in the excellence for which it has so long been celebrated.

1868 ADVERTISEMENT

1878 ADVERTISEMENT

What is interesting about these two advertisements for the MANSION HOUSE is that, with but a few word changes, they are identical even though published ten years apart. The advertisement on the left first appeared in 1868 in J.H. Schenck's booklet "A COMPLETE DESCRIPTIVE GUIDE TO LONG BRANCH, N.J." The advertisement on the right appeared in 1878 in another booklet by Schenck called "BRIGHTONS OF AMERICA." As a journalist and publisher of Long Branch books and articles, he must have kept an extensive file which he obviously used from time to time.

Congress Hall, as depicted above, was built in 1859. It became the left wing of the large Continental Hotel built in 1866. What was Congress Hall can be readily identified in any illustration of the Continental Hotel.

Possibly Pach stereograph, ca. 1865

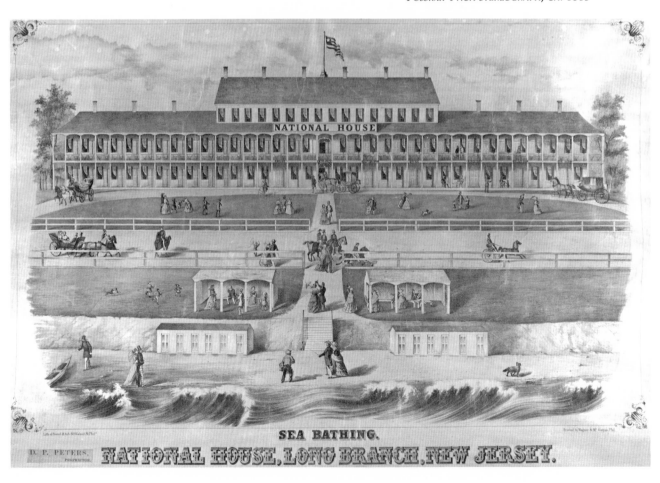

The National House became the right wing of the Continental Hotel.

ca. 1855

By 1872 the CONTINENTAL HOTEL was sold and renamed the OCEAN HOTEL. This illustration captures all the excitement and beauty of the beach, bluff and busy Ocean Avenue that made this an ideal location.

The Continental – Ocean Hotel

On Ocean Avenue, just south of the MANSION HOUSE, was the site of one of the more impressive Hotels found at Long Branch. Originally built as the CONTINENTAL HOTEL in 1866, it was sold within a few years and renamed the OCEAN HOTEL. In its day it became known as the largest summer Hotel in the United States. Its history is an interesting story. Briefly, the CONTINENTAL HOTEL was the result of joining three different buildings. In 1827 a farm house was converted into a small boarding house called the NORTH HOUSE. Samuel Cooper purchased the property in 1831 and enlarged the building into a Hotel called the COOPER HOUSE. This Hotel was sold in 1852 to Philadelphian Woolman Stokes who, in turn, again enlarged and impoved the structure and called it the NATIONAL HOUSE.

In 1859, Stokes erected another Hotel, CONGRESS HALL, a few hundred feet south of the NATIONAL HOUSE. In 1866 Stokes sold both Hotels and the property in between to a partnership of Sprague and H. A. Stokes - (the son of Woolman Stokes). A new building was then built connecting CONGRESS HALL and the NATIONAL HOUSE. The three structures became one and named the CONTINENTAL HOTEL.

This new Hotel suffered financial difficulties and, in 1872, was sold to the Leland family. With Hotels in many cities including San Francisco, Chicago, Saratoga and New York, the Lelands were the leading Hotel operators of the day. At that point in time, their new acquisition at Long Branch was renamed the OCEAN HOTEL (also called the OCEAN HOUSE at times).

One of the first comments about the new OCEAN HOUSE appeared in *FRANK LESLIE'S ILLUSTRATED NEWSPAPER* on July 26, 1873:

"The OCEAN HOUSE is, in truth, a magnificent establishment, and, confessedly, one of the fin-

89

HOTEL ARRIVALS YESTERDAY.

CONTINENTAL HOTEL,

SPRAGUE & STOKES, Proprietors.

R A Caunpiere	Chicago	M E Babech	do
R Castillen	Phila	W C Guswoer	do
R D Fralern	Louisville	J Sheldon	do
H Castrenell	Memphis	J Mott	do
W O'Neil	N J	— Cappy	do
G Castillon	N Y	— Chace	do
S W Coe	do	— Groly	
W McDapper	do	C Wendell	Chicago
W Weinberg	do	G M Fisher	St Louis
H Sidenberry	do	R Smith	do
B W Savery	do	L A Day	N Y
J H Farington	do	Miss A Detlon	do
H Buck & w	do	Miss Fitishetee	do
J Kerr	do	F S Fish	do
G Cragin	do	G W Murphy	do
W Lairnbeir	do	P Walden & w	do
J G Jaynton	do	J J Detlan	Cinn
H J Dean	do	C W Woodruff	Chicago
T Slatos	do	W M Worthington	N Y
J R Chamberlin	do	J W Bollis	do
J F Hammond	do	W C Phelps	do
A Van Saun & w	do	C W Crow	do
J A Timpson	do	M Stangisford & 1	do
H B Back & w	do	N Weehade	do
Mrs T Low	do	W D Wilson	do
E Hayman	do	W E Henessy	do
J D Ferry	do	H Moorhouse	do
W Rose	N J	J Hall	do
Miss A Craigin	do	W D Bowdie	do
Miss E Craigin	do	W Foster & w	do
T H Hungey	N Y	J F Raplee	do
H M Peak	Harristraw	Miss Styall	do
S B Solomon	N Y	J E Connah	do
S Knowlan	do	C & Meylster	do
F B Strouse	do	J B Clark	do
H Johnston	do	J Stoal	do
J Srinpeon	do	D Horigan	do
W Douets	do	D Swing	d0
G Smith	do	W H Harrison	do
J B White	do	Mrs Ardens & c	do
W C Stone	do	W C Peet	do
C B Alston & 1		G Gower	do
A S Alston		Capt Coale	do
J H McGair	N Y	W F Smith	do
L C Hopkins	Cinn	J D Vermenter	do
B F Turner	do	S Schuater	do
G R Liethster	do	W L Bleaker	do
J Wotherstone	N Y	W Lamb	do
F W Eates	do	Dr J Lynch	do
D Bates	do	J J Staff ja	do
J Millon jr	do	H Failey	do
D W Jones		J Tarry jr	do
A Johnson		C Wadger	do
E Benjamin	N Y	D B Batione	U S N
H B Lorcmain	do	W W Johnson	Ind
J R Johnson	Phila	J F Towell	Portsmouth
E Hoore	N J	C Beardell & w	N J
A D Breackenhoff	N Y	Miss E Beardell	do
G C Dey		L Van Dowen	do
W C Langdor		E W Robcins	do
C G Keys		J Forrey	do
C R Gregon		W A Davis	Louisville Ky
W A Gregon		K Marshall	
E Kaker	Brooklyn	W Johnson	
D Carpenter		G A Woolley	
W Oleyn		J E Stewart	
J H Weber	Chicago	W C Laphafrer	
H Scott	N Y	F D Maziha	
M Smith		W J Walker	Washington
J S Lowery & s		B Haywood	Pa
G A Dickson	N Y	P E Chase	Phila
P Tale	do	W L Marshall	do
R A Whitely	N J	G P Coningham	do
Thos Whitely	do	J B Crimeny	Utica
J W Conglan	N Y		

AT THE CONTINENTAL STABLES.

Isaac Marsh, N. J., 1 pair sorrel carriage horses.

J. H. Bedle, N. Y., 1 pair fancy matched road horses, very fast.

Jos. Naylor, N. Y., 1 pair fancy matched road horses, fine team.

S. D. Mills, Philadelphia, 1 fine sorrel road horse.

A. L. Maurey, N. Y., 1 pair fancy matched carriage horses.

G. H. Chapman, N. J., 1 pair bay carriage horses.

J. R. McConnell, N. Y., 1 pair fancy matched carriage horses, stylish.

T. Westcott, Trenton, 1 pair bay carriage horses, fine team.

S. W. A. Ward, N. Y., 1 pair bay carriage horses.

— Patton, N. Y., 1 poney, very small.

J. R. Sprague, 1 fine saddle sorrel horse.

— Lovett, Philadelphia, 1 bay mare for road.

H. S. Morange, N. Y., 1 very stylish grey road horse, and a unique jump-seat wagon, very attractive.

Dr. W. C. Otterson, Brooklyn, 1 fine road horse.

Charles Harkness, Philadelphia, 1 pair carriage horses.

H. G. Eastman, Poughkeepsie, a splendid four-in-hand team, with a stylish equipage.

B. B. Hotchkiss, N. Y., a very stylish four-in-hand team—a magnificent turn out.

S. W. Coe, N. Y., an elegant pair of black carriage horses.

L. L. Abbott, Va., a very fast grey horse.

A. C. Laurence, N. Y., 1 black mare, very fast.

— Matthews, N. Y., 1 pair fancy matched carriage horses 1 pair bay ponies, very handsome.

J. Becker, Philadelphia, 1 pair bay carriage horses.

W. H. Conover, jr., Freehold, 1 grey road horse, very fast; 1 pair bay carriage horses, a fine team; a very handsome carriage, built by Captain W. Furman, Freehold. N.J., equal in appearance to anything of the kind on the shore.

Sprague & Stokes, 2 pairs fine carriage horses.

B. W. Blanchard, N. Y., 1 pair very handsome brown carriage horses, 1 bay road horse, fast.

John Mortimer, N. Y., 1 pair bay carriage horses.

C. Minzeshoimer, N. Y., 1 pair black carriage horses.

Mrs. Dr. Moffett, N. Y., 1 pair bay carriage horses, 1 black poney and phaeton.

J. C. West, N. Y., 1 pair fancy matched carriage horses, fast; 1 bay poney, 1 brown horse, said to be the fastest horse at Long Branch.

G. H. Jones, N. Y., 1 pair fancy matched carriage horses, 1 mottled road horse, fast.

G. Green, N. Y., 1 pair elegant bay carriage horses.

J. B. Lalor, Trenton, 1 pair roan road horses, stylish and good travellers.

F. Camblos, N. Y., 1 pair stylish black carriage horses.

A. R. Little, Philadelphia, 1 pair fine sorrel carriage horses.

J. B. Olcott, Washington, D. C., 4 pairs matched horses, and stylish equipages, 3 splendid saddle horses, and a number of fine single horses, on livery. The horses and equipments will compare favorably with the private establishments at Long Branch.

The LONG BRANCH DAILY NEWS *often published lists of the latest hotel arrivals along with a description of the guests' horses. The hotels often had their own stables.*

DAILY NEWS.

LONG BRANCH, N. J., AUGUST 6, 1866.

THE CONTINENTAL BALL.

BEAUTY AND FASHION ON "DRESS PARADE."

Grand Display of Silks, Diamonds, Bright Eyes, Flowers and Good Manners.

The Ball at the *Continental* on Friday night last, brief notice of which we gave in Satu day's NEWS, was decidedly the grandest affair of the kind ever witnessed at Long Branch.— There is now congregated here a greater number of wealthy and fashionable people from all quarters of the world, than ever before graced this shore, and there is no other room in this country so well calculated to display all this wealth and beauty as the spacious and airy dining room of the *Continental*. All the tables had been removed, and the chairs had been arranged against the walls, leaving ample room for the ladies to swing their broad skirts in the dance at their own sweet will, and for once giving the gentlemen no pretext for railing at the circumference of their dresses.

At ten o'clock FAERBER's splendid band struck up the "Continental March," the doors were thrown open, and the gaily dressed ladies and gentlemen trooped in, and soon formed a continuous circle in a grand promenade.— The scene at this time was dazzling. Silks, Pearls, Diamonds, Flowers and Boquets fringed the inside of the circle of gentlemen clothed in conventional black, forming, as they moved under the brilliant gas lights, one of the most beautiful sights ever witnessed.

But little time was given for conversation. Sets were rapidly formed, and dance after dance followed in quick succession, until the small hours threatened to become longer ones, and yet the dancers seemed to show no signs of weariness, owing, in a great measure, no doubt, to the delicious coolness of the room throughout the evening, and the inspiring music of the band.

About one o'clock an intermission was given, and the guests partook of a handsome collation provided by the proprietors of the Continental. The table before it was attacked presented a beautiful appearance.

It would be impossible were our sheet quadrupled in size, to notice all the notabilities who were present. We commenced taking notes of the many striking costumes that were constantly passing us, but soon became bewildered in the mysteries of morie-antique, tulle, point lace, and cluny, and broke down before we fairly commenced. Subsequently, with the kind assistance of two or three ladies who had dropped in to view the scene, we obt ined the following, which we confidently present to the public as "official," at least, so far as the dresses are concerned:

Miss Mary Mason, Philadelphia, wore a pink silk skir*t*, white puffed waist; very attractive

Mrs. Wallace, Cincinnatti, wore a garnet-colored silk, and white lace shawl; elegant diamond jewelry.

Miss Anne Clouse, Boston, wore a white alpaca, trimmed with blue velvet, high corsage; very neat. One of the youthful belles gracing the ball.

Mrs. Coe, New York, was dressed in pure white muslin displaying much refinement of style.

Mrs. Westcott, Trenton, wore a pink silk, with lace overskirt, beautifully trimmed with white spangles; attracted much attention.

Mrs. Stitt, New York, wore a figured alpacca, elaborately trimmed with black velvet.

Mrs. Caswell, New York, wore a beautiful plum-colored silk.

Miss Parker, Pittsburgh, wore a white muslin skirt, trimmed with scarlet.

Mrs. General Meylart, Tarry'own, wore a green silk dress, black lace shawl, high corsag , with point lace; hair trimmed with pearls; very elegant costume, displaying excellent taste.

Mrs. Freeborn, New York, wore a grey moire antique, trimmed with white point lace, white point *epplique* shawl; a profuse display of costly diamonds; very stately and elegant.

Mrs. Judge Roosevelt, New York, was plainly dressed, but her stately and elegant manners attracted much attention

Miss Combs, Red Bank, wore a white dress; very chaste style.

Miss Lida Conover, Long Branch, wore a light blue silk, low corsage, puffed tulle waist, trimmed with point lace; very beautiful.

Mrs. Antram, New York, wore a green silk dress.

Miss Freeborn, New York, wore a white mohair, trimmed with *cluny* lace; pearl ornaments.

Mrs. Bullock, Mount Holly, wore a black grenadine dress.

Mrs. Benedict, New York, wore a lovely shade of mauve moire antique, point lace shawl, and an elaborate display of diamonds.

Miss Mall, Philadelphia, wore a white mohair, trimmed with scarlet; hair dressed with scarlet flowers.

Miss Mason, Philadelphia, wore a pearl-colored silk, puffed illusion waist; hair trimmed with flowers.

Miss Reed, Mount Holly, wore a white mohair, cherry trimmings.

Miss Ella Mason, wore a maize-colored dress, with puffed tulle waist; hair and dress trimmed with flowers. A very attractive and stylish belle.

Mrs. Sprague, the charming hostess of the *Continental*, wore an emerald green silk, trimmed with black guimpure lace, and a rich black thread lace shawl; hair dressed with flowers. Her amiable disposition and brilliant conversation and manners made her welcome in every circle.

Mrs. Nye, Cincinnatti, was richly dressed in green silk, white point lace shawl, and diamond jewelry.

Mrs. Dr. Darling, New York, was very chastely dressed in pure white, with scarlet flowers.

Miss Wallace, Cincinnatti, dress corn color trimmed with scarlet, attracted much attention by her graceful dancing.

Mrs. Goodyear, a very stylish dress, "moon-on-the-lake" silk, trimmed with festoons of scarlet velvet and *cluny* lace; hair dressed with corals.

Mrs. L. Fassitt, Philadelphia, wore a black moire antique, black lace trimmings; a handsome display of diamonds.

Mrs. Blanchard, New York, wore a plum-colored silk, low corsage, point lace cape.

A lady whose name we did not learn, attracted much attention by her tall and graceful figure. She wore a blue silk slip, Swiss overdress; hair very tastefully dressed with pearls.

A party of elegantly-dressed ladies and gentlemen, who arrived by the evening train of cars. among them Mrs. E. A. Stevens, were present, and enjoying the festivities.

Mrs. West, New York, wore a light blue silk, elegantly trimmed, and very stylish; a brilliant display of pearls and diamonds.

Miss Ferguson, New York, wore a white barege, trimmed with blue, and a very novel basque. She attracted much attention by her graceful style.

Mrs. Camblos, of New York, was very tastefully dressed.

Mrs. Baker, of Philadelphia, graced the room with her presence, but just at this moment, having lost our interpreters, we did not dare to attempt a description of her costume.

There were quite a number of young misses present, who were dressed regardless of expense, and with much taste and beauty.

Thanks to the accomplished managers, everything passed off in the best style, and in the most pleasant manner.

This article creates an impressive word picture of "Beauty and Fashion on Dress Parade" at the CONTINENTAL HOTEL.

91

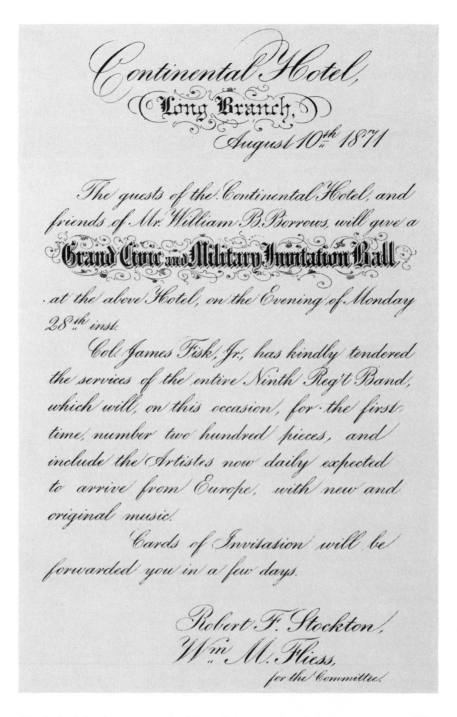

Typical of the dances was the "Grand Civic and Military Invitation Ball"
held in the CONTINENTAL HOTEL in August of 1871.
Colonel James Fisk, Jr. was involved and "tendered the services
of the entire Ninth Reg't Band." The beautifully engraved
invitation reveals more information about the Ball.

The OCEAN HOTEL of the Lelands.

est Hotels in Long Branch. Those who have never visited it, may form some idea of the dimensions when we state that, to make a circuit of the building three times, involves a journey of a mile. The vista provided by the veranda, with its long lines of flower-baskets, pendant between the pillars, is charming in the extreme; while the beautiful lawn and croquet-ground in front are most attractive, and give full scope to the fresh, pure air that comes up from the sea.

It has always struck us that, in the case of Hotels, the kitchen and the pantry form very fair criteria as to the establishment generally. The kitchen...is one of the loftiest and finest we have ever seen, while the pantry — if a series of underground establishments may be termed such — is truly on a most efficient and magnificent scale. The dining room is a section of a palace. Three enormous vases of flowers make it redolent of perfume, and gratify the eye with a wilderness of odorous rainbows. The drawing-room, too, is truly regal. What a meadow of carpet! All this is quite familiar to the *habitues* of Long Branch, as many a sweet young heart knows full well.

The table, of course, is admirable, and all the rooms and appointments superb. Three times a day a full band discourses sweet music on the lawn, and every evening after supper there is a concert and dancing, so that there is no lack of amusement or comfort."

This interior view of the OCEAN HOTEL's dining room with its waiters standing by gives some idea of the vast potential seating capacity.

PACH STEREOGRAPH #101B, CA. 1874

93

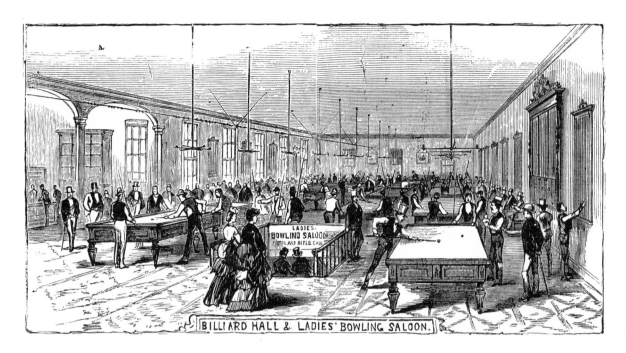

BILLIARD HALL & LADIES' BOWLING SALOON.

The game of billiards was a popular indoor sport in many hotels for men, while women were attracted to bowling. This view shows the facilities provided by the OCEAN HOTEL.
FRANK LESLIE'S ILLUSTRATED NEWSPAPER, July 6, 1872

This is a far cry from the comments published in the *KNICKERBOCKER* thirty-five years earlier, in 1838, in which the author of that particular article lamented there was little to do at the Branch and, as a result, there were "some very heavy hours accumulating upon our hands."

An extremely detailed and enlightening description of the OCEAN HOTEL appeared in the fascinating guidebook published by R. F. and C. P. Dearborn in 1874 and called "What To Do In Long Branch." Curiously, it appears that the Dearborns either read the previous article published in July of 1873 — or — they actually wrote it for *FRANK LESLIE'S ILLUSTRATED NEWSPAPER* because a number of sentences are identical in both of the entire publications!

"The OCEAN HOTEL; the property of Charles and Warren Leland, whose names are household words among the first families of America as the leading Hotel managers of the Continent.

This mammoth establishment is located on Ocean Avenue, and with its magnificent grounds embraces a space of twelve acres in extent, and covering an entire square of the town from avenue to avenue.

It is the largest summer Hotel in the world. Of all the Hotels at the Branch it is the most conveniently located, situated as it is within a short distance of the village, surrounded on either side by Hotels, and commanding from its piazzas a view of the ocean and beach which is magnificent beyond description.

Statistics are generally rather figurative, you know, but our readers may rely upon those given below. The Hotel accommodates upwards of 1,200 guests. Length, of piazzas, over 2,000 feet. The dining-room is 250 feet by 58 feet, and 20 feet high, and is unequalled in size, and is adorned with fountains. The piazzas which surrounds the house is one-third of a mile long. The Hotel employs 150 waiters and 28 cooks.

The internal arrangements of the house are as complete as it is possible for money, enterprise and experience to make them. Its drawing-room is a section of a palace, with its carpets as soft as the meadow, and of fabulous price, and its costly chandeliers.

Three times a day the orchestra of Wm. Keating discourses sweet music on the lawn, and every evening after supper there is a concert and dancing, so that there is no lack of amusement and comfort.

An extensive bowling-alley for ladies and large and well lighted billiard-rooms are located within the grounds and attached to the Hotel.

The vista presented by the verandah, with its long lines of flower baskets pendent between the pillars, is charming in the extreme; while the beautiful lawn and croquet ground in front are most attractive, and give free scope to the fresh, pure air that comes up from the sea.

The lawn is left free of shrubbery that the grand sweep of ocean view may not be marred; but in the extensive court-yard behind the Hotel, no less than 250 new trees have been set out this spring to adorn the grounds. A gallery, covered throughout, is now finished at the back of the Hotel, which will furnish a covered promenade the entire circuit of the buildings, a distance of one-fourth of a mile. Hanging baskets of flowers, with French lights upon alternate pillars, will decorate this gallery. The length of the promenade, and the convenience of the fractional division of a mile, will make it attractive for gentlemen who may wish to emulate the feats of Mr. Weston and Mr. Bennett, under cover, and with a constant throng of enthusiastic spectators. A few rooms have been added to the capacity of the OCEAN HOTEL, which before readily provided lodgings for

1,200 hundred persons. Frescoing, painting, and new furniture comprises the other improvements. In the Fall, it is proposed to begin the erection of an extensive additional wing, the ground floor of which will contain 10 stores opening upon Main street, and having also a front on the pleasant court-yard of the Hotel. These will secure to the lady guests the most tempting opportunity to gratify their taste for expenditure even in rainy weather.

One of the chief features of the Leland cuisine is the fish from the private fishery of the Hotel, and nowhere are the finny tribe served up more deliciously.

M. Jules Harder is the chief cook, and he knows what he is doing. He studied under his father with the Lelands, has some sixteen years with pots, pans, kettles, and their contents, and although a young man, has been offered the mastership of the kitchen of the new Palace Hotel in San Francisco, which will be, when completed, the largest and best appointed in the world. M. Harder is attired in the conventional cap and apron of the cuisine. He has eight men cooks and ten women to assist him, and is

DINING UNDER DIFFICULTIES.

Dining under difficulties was, indeed, often a problem that had little to do with the menu. These young ladies, after properly arranging their hoops and flaring skirts and seating themselves, left no room at the dinner table for their gentlemen friends.

95

Long Branch Daily News, August 21, 1873

"Bathing Hour at Long Branch – Scene in Front of the OCEAN HOTEL."
FRANK LESLIE'S ILLUSTRATED NEWSPAPER, SEPTEMBER 1, 1877

A SAND BATH ON THE BEACH.

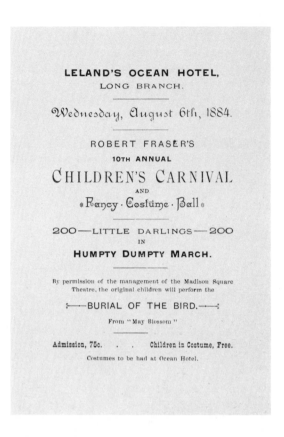

Through the years children enjoyed many of the amusements that were provided for them. They even had their own Fancy Costume Ball for over ten years. In 1884 there were "200 little darlings" in a special Humpty Dumpty March. That must have been something to see. Just north of the Hotel there was a children's railroad (pulled by a donkey) that kept many youngsters entertained.

"Ocean Hotel, Children's Pleasure Railroad."
New Jersey Stereoscopic View Co., #82c, 1873

monarch over ten separate furnaces and three broiling fires. The latter point is noticeable, for one broiler is set apart for fish, another for beef-steaks, and another for mutton chops, so that there may be no mixture of flavor, and that the flavor of each meat may be preserved. Charcoal is used for chops, and other fuels for steaks and fish. In the right-hand corner is a large brick oven for baking potatoes, and at the extreme end are two large copper cauldrons used for stock boilers. The space between is occupied by a line of cooking-ranges, extending 75 feet across the entire width of the house. A large table is set in the center of which a Bain-Marie or hot water bath is sunk, in which sauces are kept warm after they have been made and seasoned. A potato-masher nine inches in diameter and the machine that slices 'Long Branch potatoes,' are among the culinary curiosities of the place.

Mr. Van B. Leland, who is the steward of the Hotel, finds it no easy matter to provide this army of cooks with sufficient food to keep them going. They would eat their heads off if they did not get enough food, and the amount that passes through their hands is tremendous. In the height of the season 900 lbs. of fish, 1,500 of meat and four barrels of potatoes are required, daily, while chickens come in by the hundreds and vegetables by the dozen basketfuls per day.

We have seen where the pieces de resistance come from, but what about the pies and dessert? These belong to another department, and to investigate their origin we must visit the bakery, which is situated on the ground floor. If the French are the best cooks, the Italians are the best bakers. It is to them that we owe the invention of macaroni, and Signors Godfrey and Dessori, the chief baker and confectioner, are Italians. Their vaulted abode reminds one of the logia of the villages on the Via Cornici,

and they have fitted up an alcove with Italian taste, and have a couple of pet robins hopping about. Six assistants help them to make ice cream, pies, pastry, cakes and bread, and they use three barrels of flour and 400 eggs a day.

The remainder of the basement under the dining-hall is occupied by the meat, vegetable, and store-rooms, the latter of which is as well stocked as a corner grocery; the laundry rooms, with twenty-four stationary tubs, steam drying-horses, and an ironing furnace which will heat thirty irons. Here, also, are situated the servants' hall and the dining-room for nurses and children, as well as ice-rooms, fitted up for keeping milk, butter, and eggs, equipped with refrigerators whose economy would astonish the directors of the Knickerbocker Ice Company.

The Ocean table is set with a well-chosen menu, the leading features being changed every day, while standard dishes are kept on continuously. There is no attempt to serve up two hundred and seventy-five dishes, all of which taste of sawdust, garlic, and grease, but a sufficient variety is provided, and each article is good in kind and good in cooking. M. Harder sends in a first-class French dinner; when you sip your coffee, you feel that you have dined. Room-clerk Is Mr. O. J. Brown, and the office-clerk, Mr. George F. Putney."[1]

The OCEAN HOTEL suffered all sorts of problems in its last years of existence. The photograph that follows shows that the right wing of the hotel had been removed, reducing the size of the hotel's capacity by one third. These were not good years for the hotel business. The final blow came in the summer of 1902. The current proprietor vanished, leaving debts and unpaid bills. The hotel never reopened and was finally torn down in 1905.

A typical notice in the Long Branch Daily News *lists the* Metropolitan Hotel's *latest arrivals. On this particular day in 1866, the majority of guests came from New York.*

This list from the Metropolitan Hotel's *Stables, as usual, describes the newly-arrived horses and identifies their individual owners. As active equestrians, a number of these hotel guests often brought more than two horses.*

The Metropolitan Hotel

Pach stereograph #9, 1873

The Metropolitan Hotel

A large and imposing L-shaped structure, the Metropolitan Hotel, located on the north corner of Cooper and Ocean Avenue, was built in 1854 by Samuel and Joseph H. Cooper. A Mr. Vandyke and the Coopers operated the hotel for the first two seasons. Then Joseph H. Cooper and Thomas W. Cooper (son of Samuel Cooper) became proprietors until 1865. In that year, The New York Times published an article called "Our Watering Places" which described some of the hotels of Long Branch. This article is one of the earliest references to the Metropolitan Hotel.

"The hotels are fourteen in number. Of these, (stated the reporter) about a dozen are called "first-class." I should not call them so, using my own judgement; but I suppose it is the price that regulates it, though in that case the whole fourteen are "first-class," for they all charge $4 a day, or $21 per week. There are some farm-houses and cottages, I understand, where the board is as low as $18. The really first-class hotels are the Mansion House, the Metropolitan, Congress Hall, the United States, the Pavilion, the Bath, Howland's and the Lawn - and this ought to be enough, in all conscience, but it isn't. These are almost always overcrowded.

The hotels, I conclude from personal observation, are the first two named. They are the largest, the most elegant, and have the choicest representation of fashion, beauty, wealth and refinement.

You see I put refinement last; it is usually in a woeful minority at all summer resorts. I cannot better indicate the real status of the hotels, in a way to enable a stranger to chose to his liking than by characterizing the Mansion House as the "Astor" of Long Branch, and the Metropolitan as the "Fifth-Avenue." Though their terms are lower than the Newport hotels, their fare is better. It is good and that is enough. Pretty much everything is "growded" in sight of the house - from chickens to cucumbers. The Metropolitan is supported on the left by a cornfield big enough for a city youngster to get lost in irrecoverably, I should think.

The amusements - I mean, of course, the indoor amusements - are varied. There is dancing in the parlors of the leading hotels every night, with good bands of music; and some of these parties are very gay. They are open to all comers, but, for obvious reasons, the participants are usually the guests of the hotel at which they dance. There was a grand "first of the season" hop at the Metropolitan on Thursday evening at which the display of toilettes was quite up to the requirements of the age. It was a "perfect crush," and brilliant in the highest degree."[1]

All of these affairs were not exactly "brilliant in the highest degree" in each hotel in spite of the crowds. Take, for example, these notes regarding a grand hop in August of 1865:

"The weekly grand hop at the Metropolitan took place on Wednesday evening. Great are the complaints of the ladies at the scarcity of young gentlemen, *au fait* in the waltz and the Lanciers.

The Mansion House grand hop on Friday evening was a very elegant though much crowded affair.

The hotels are still thronged. When ten go away, twenty come to take their places. Cots and sofas are in steady demand, and windowsills are wanted at the old quotations."[2]

Music played an important part in the daily entertainment of hotel guests. In 1872, the Metropolitan engaged Beck's popular band from Philadelphia for the entire season. It offered open air concerts on the Lawn both in the morning and the evening for the public to enjoy. Also, every evening guests danced at their own private hop in the hotel's parlor.

In the season of 1866, a portion of the hotel was rebuilt. Samuel Laird later became a new partner with Joseph H. Cooper. Then, for a while, Cooper left and became associated with Congress Hall (which became part of the Continental Hotel). However, in 1873, he returned to the Metropolitan as Manager. That became a new era for the hotel as was duly noted by the local press.

"Since last season this hotel has changed owners , and it is now under the management of Mr. Joseph H. Cooper, who built it in 1854, and was, for some years thereafter, the successful proprietor.

In passing through the hotel we find that the entire building has been thoroughly overhauled and renovated. Many of the rooms have been entirely refurnished, as many as one hundred suits of new furniture having been purchased for that purpose. The large dining room has received its share of attention, every article of furniture therein being new.

The Billiard Hall which has become somewhat impaired, is being refitted, and placed in the very best of order, so that those who desire it may enjoy this refined pastime in the pleasantest manner.

The crop of grass and weeds, which had taken possession of the walks and carriageways around the hotel, has been rooted out - in fact the entire hotel grounds are being put in complete order. For little children, the fine shaded lawn in the rear of the hotel will be the pleasantest along the shore. An improvement in this part of the hotel and grounds is, that the unsightly whitewash, which formerly covered the rear part of the hotel and out buildings, has given place to a plentiful supply of nice white paint. Those who know Mr. Cooper will have no fear about the management of the Metropolitan. He is a hotelkeeper of no small experience, having been born in a hotel and having remained in one ever since.

Taking everything into consideration, we do not see why the Metropolitan may not be one of the most popular hotels in Long Branch."[3]

Changes, repairs, renovation, and expansion were an ongoing part of the hotel business. After all, one had to keep up with the local competition. By 1874 the Metropolitan had a capacity of 600 patrons and was charging $3 to $5 a day for accommodations.

"If nothing else should make the Metropolitan successful, it could hardly fail to be so, in such excellent and experienced hands as Manager Cooper. The house has all the comforts of home, cosy parlors, extensive Lawns, and piazzas."[4]

In the beginning of the following season of 1875, a New York Times reporter made this observation:

"The Metropolitan, which belongs to Dr. Conover, and which has been managed for so many years by the Coopers of Long Branch, has been the scene of considerable change. It has been so covered with verandahs that its appearance is absolutely new, and the old frequenters would hardly know it. The topmost rooms have been greatly enlarged, and I understand that here, too, the Centennial occupies the thoughts of the management so greatly that in all probability the lower floor will be remodeled, and the parlors, diningroom and offices will be transformed. There is a new manager, Mr. W.

W. Palmer, who keeps the MAGNOLIA HOUSE at St. Augustine, Fla. Dr. Conover, who spends his Winter there every year, imported him to Long Branch."[5]

In spite of a successful business operation for over twenty years, surprisingly, there are comparatively few detailed accounts of the daily social activities at this hotel. It appears the establishments at the southern portion of Ocean Avenue enjoyed much more publicity on a day to day basis and, as a result their social events are well documented. As a result of the lack of publicity, even illustrations of the METROPOLITAN HOTEL are scarce.

The hotel was ultimately destroyed by fire on April 25, 1876. Within two years a new hotel called the BRIGHTON was erected on that site. A much smaller building, it was popular in its day.

LONG BRANCH.

METROPOLITAN HOTEL,

(BEACH DRIVE NORTH, 3.)

COOPER & LAIRD, Proprietors.

This house is conveniently located near the depots and upon the bluff, with a fine view South and West.

The Capacity is for 600 Guests.

Terms, - - - $25.00 per Week.

Open until October 1st.

BECK'S PHILADELPHIA BAND is engaged for the Season.

FINE BATHING FACILITIES

AND

Other auxiliaries of a FIRST-CLASS HOUSE.

A COMPLETE LIVERY ESTABLISHMENT
is connected with the Hotel.

SUNDAY, AUGUST 18, 1889.

SOUP.
Mock Turtle

FISH.
Boiled Sea Bass, Anchovy sauce

RELISHES.
Chow Chow   Cold Slaw   Mixed Pickles

Worcestershire Sauce   Olives

COLD DISHES.
Roast Beef   Ham   Beef Tongue

ENTREES.
Fried Soft Shell Crabs au Naturel

Ris de Veau aux Petits Pois

Stewed Mushrooms au Madere

Peaches with Rice, a la Conde

ROAST.
Ham, Champagne sauce

Ribs of Beef   Spring Lamb, Mint sauce   Philadelphia Spring Chicken

VEGETABLES.
New Potatoes   Lima Beans   Mashed Potatoes

Green Corn   Boiled Rice   Stewed Tomatoes

PASTRY.
Floating Island Pudding

Peach Pie   Cocoanut Custard Pie   Wine Jelly   Assorted Cakes

DESSERT.
Ice Cream   Almonds   English Walnuts   Raisins

Pecans   Crackers   Cheese

Watermelon   Confectionery

COFFEE   TEA

This BRIGHTON HOTEL menu was typical of the period (1889). With such a wide variety of choices, dining was undoubtedly a special social activity enjoyed by everyone. In the delightful engraving of the hotel, a young woman and a gentleman can be seen playing a friendly game of tennis on the front lawn.

104

Alexandre & Masters'

Ponce de Leon

Riding Academy

From ST. AUGUSTINE, FLA.,

—AT THE—

HOTEL · BRIGHTON,

LONG BRANCH, N. J.

TERMS.

20 LESSONS	$30.00
12 LESSONS	20.00
6 LESSONS	12.00
SINGLE LESSONS	2.50
ROAD LESSONS, one person	6.00
ROAD LESSONS, for clubs of three or more	4.00

EXERCISE

20 ROAD RIDES	$50.00
SINGLE RIDE, 2 hours	3.00

$1.00 PER HOUR FOR EXTRA TIME.

Horses taken in Board, per month		$30.00
Hire of Saddle { per month		10.00
{ per ride		.50

Horses to hire by the month or season.

Horses carefully trained and broken to the saddle for Ladies and Gentlemen.

Horses bought, sold or exchanged on commission.

This booklet (1889), from the BRIGHTON HOTEL, shows the cost of boarding one's horses. This was an important consideration to many visitors to Long Branch. Most of the hotels maintained their own stables.

Brighton Hotel

The BRIGHTON HOTEL survived for a number of years. By 1900 the hotel was enlarged and completely rebuilt. Like most hotels, it had several owners and, in later years, was know as the HOTEL AMBASSADOR.

On January 7, 1930, just twenty-four hours after it was sold to the Sedgwick Manor Realty Corporation, of New York City, the hotel was leveled by what was called a suspicious fire. Aided by a 30-mile an hour gale, flames totally destroyed the three-and-a-half story frame structure in just five hours.

THE „OLD ATLANTIC".

An artist's rendering of the original ATLANTIC HOTEL as it might have looked around 1867. This illustration is from a souvenir booklet entitled "Views of Long Branch." It was an advertising piece published (ca. 1885) by Chisholm Brothers of Maine for Fred Hoey's Hollywood Hotel and Cottages.

ATLANTIC HOTEL,
A. CRISTALAR, Proprietor.

Tobias Lyon	N Y	L Gotthold	do
Louis Bernstein	do	J Rosenberg	do
M Steinhardt	do	J Mooney	do
L D Leman	do	S Heillman	do
John C Jeffries	do	F Arke	Baltimore
L Schlesinger	do	H Strauss	do
M Naumberg	do	Mr Stark	do
M Cohen	do	L Piek	do
A M Cristalar	do	L Scharff	Vicksburg
G Pach	do	— Bautim	Memphis
C Weis	do	A Cohen	do
Geo L Ayer	do	Jacob Lewn	Lafayette Ind
S Hahn	do	B Loeb	Mobile
H Eisfelder	do	B Forene	Phila
S Truhart	do	J Langsdonson	do

The latest arrivals at the ATLANTIC HOTEL were reported in the LONG BRANCH DAILY NEWS, August 6, 1866. Noted photographer, Gustavus Pach, is listed among the hotel guests. The following year he opened his studio on the grounds of the CONTINENTAL HOTEL.

A rare view of the Arlington House formerly the old Atlantic Hotel.

Atlantic Hotel – Arlington House – Long Branch Excursion House – East End Hotel

The little known history of this particular structure, the ATLANTIC HOTEL, is like a frustrating family genealogy - a bewildering and twisting puzzle lacking many informative details. It is, nevertheless, an example that cannot be passed over with just a simple reference. The most northern of the Grand Hotels of Long Branch, through the years this hotel was known by four different names.

While not one of the most impressive hotels, nevertheless the original ATLANTIC HOTEL (later the ARLINGTON HOUSE, and still later, the EAST END HOTEL) was popular and did cater to an important segment of the busy hotel scene -the excursionists. The hotel offered numerous social events similar to the other fashionable establishments. While many individuals spent a week or more at this hotel, the larger crowd who came to the Branch for little more than a daily visit found this location to their liking.

Situated at the northern end of Ocean Avenue (on what is now Seven Presidents Park), it was within walking distance of the New Jersey Southern Rail Road's Depot. In later years there was a Railroad stop called the Excursion Platform actually located on the extreme western end of the hotel's property.

Alexander M. Cristalar signed a contract on September 19, 1861 with John Bell, a Long Branch Carpenter and Builder, to erect and finish a "new Building for a Hotel" under the direction of the architect, Henry Fernbach. It was to be erected "on a certain lot of ground" owned by Cristalar and was to be finished by April 15, 1862.

On the 24th of December in 1863 another agreement was made by Cristalar with carpenter Benjamin Coles to add an addition to the southern wing of this new structure called the ATLANTIC HOTEL. It was a major addition measuring

"20 feet six inches by 42 feet square and 3 stories high."

As most of the hotels provided Grand Balls and Hops and musical programs as part of their contribution to the social activities of their patrons, so did the ATLANTIC HOTEL. On the evening of August 4, 1866, for example, the hotel provided its guests with one of these popular events which, of course, allowed the men to socialize and the women to display their finery.

"The second grand Hop at the ATLANTIC HOTEL, on Saturday last, was a recherche affair and was attended by a brilliant throng, comprising beauty, wealth and fashion. The highest expectations of those that attended this Hop were fully realized, and the hall of Epicurus was filled with a happy throng of devotees of Terpischore, who, attired in the most magnificent and costly manner, whirling through the mazes of the quadrilles and polkas, waltzes and lancers, (as well as Marches, Gallops and Schottisches). The music mingled in indescribable harmony with the roar of the breakers upon the shore, the glitter of diamonds, combined to form a grand and perfect panorama, that will not soon be forgotten by those who had the pleasure of participating in it.

At 9 o'clock the doors of the airy dining hall were thrown open, the Band filling the room with its sweetest strains, and the long line of promenaders filed into the hall and the dances, twenty-four in number, were kept up until a very late hour.

During the intermission, an excellent supper was provided by the gentlemanly host, Mr. Cristalar, at which was served all the palate could desire."[1]

In the following summer of 1867 it was reported:

"...this popular house has been enlarged and re-furnished, and is delightfully situated off the northern portion of the Long Branch Beach, and is one of the best houses on the shore. Every care taken to conduce to the welfare of the guests. A. Cristalar, Prop."[2]

An editorial from the same newspaper stated:

"We received a very polite reception from Mr. Cristalar, the proprietor of this house, which is one of the most complete hotels we ever saw. Improvements are constantly going forward, looking to the elegant comfort of its guests and greater efficiency of management. It is capable of accommodating 500 persons, and is chiefly, if not entirely, held for the use of persons of the Hebrew faith, and mostly those of the greatest wealth and character. Its success is assured."[3]

While there are numerous discrepancies in many of these published comments, to a great degree they do present a basis for fact. Journalist J.H. Schenck, in 1868, offered this statement.

"This is the farthest north, of the hotels on the bluff, being about a half a mile from the depot. It was built by Aaron Christalar in 1861-62, and rebuilt in '66. Capacity: some two hundred and fifty guests. The building is very near the edge of the bluff, with fine bathing and other facilities. A band of music is in attendance throughout the season. The house is well kept, and is patronized very largely by adherents of the Jewish faith. Mr. Christalar, the original proprietor, still owns and conducts this hotel."[4]

On February 18, 1869, Alexander M. Cristalar and his wife sold the land, buildings and improvements to Mr. & Mrs. Frederick R. Rickenberg for $46,000. A notice appeared in the NEW YORK TRIBUNE:

"ATLANTIC HOTEL, Long Branch, N.J. - This house, having changed owners, has been refitted throughout, and is now open. Terms very moderate. Catering in the German and American style..."[5]

On April 29, 1871, the Rickenbergs leased the land and the Hotel to one Lewis Stine. Because of apparent financial difficulties, it was purchased by Solomon Jessurun on May 25, 1871, as the result of a Sheriff's Sale. By October 9, 1871, Mr. Jessurun sold it and the hotel was back in the hands of Alexander M. Cristalar!

It was probably renamed the ARLINGTON HOUSE in 1871 and was still located on the corner of Ocean Avenue and the new Troutman Avenue. The hotel was sold once again and "thoroughly refitted, renovated and refurnished" and appears to have reopened on July 1, 1873, as the LONG BRANCH EXCURSION HOUSE.

While the above advertisement was published on July 3, 1873, in the LONG BRANCH NEWS, a rather lengthy article appeared in the same newspaper the previous day describing this "new" hotel:

"The building formerly known as the AR-LINGTON HOUSE, together with the grounds (consisting of twenty acres) surrounding it, has been purchased by the New Jersey Southern Railroad, and henceforth is to be known as the LONG BRANCH EXCURSION HOUSE.

The old building has been entirely renovated and enlarged without regard to expense, the company being determined to have a house capable of accommodating the large excursion parties which every season visit the Branch.

The entire house has been furnished in such a manner as to ensure the comfort of those who shall visit it. A ball-room, large enough for two hundred couples, is among the attractions of the house.

This opens directly on the broad verandahs, wither the guests may retire to enjoy the cool sea breeze after having "tipped the light fantastic." On the beautiful lawn, almost as level as a floor, children may romp, ladies and gents play croquet, while those who love the more vigorous sport of base-ball, may engage in that

popular pastime. Indeed, this house seems to furnish every facility for every enjoyment which an excursion party might desire.

The management of the EXCURSION HOUSE has been entrusted to Mr. F.S. Freeze, while Mr. J.H. Carpenter of Philadelphia, is one of the Excursion Ticket Agents. We think that this new enterprise will supply a want long felt here, and we are sure all will join with us in saying that the managers of the New Jersey Southern deserve great credit for discovering this public want and for their energy in supplying it.

And, furthermore, we are sure that the enterprise cannot fail of success in a financial point of view, for already has there been one excursion - the beginning of many, we hope.

This excursion came down last Thursday and was under the auspices of the ticket agents attached to the Baltimore and Ohio, New York and Erie, and Pennsylvania Central Railroads, who are stationed at Philadelphia.

The party arrived at the Branch about 11 A.M. and spent the remainder of the day in bathing, wandering on the beach, dancing, and partaking of the good things of this house as they were set forth by Manager Freeze. At 6 P.M. the party left for home highly pleased with their day's enjoyment."[6]

Now comes the real confusing part of this particular story. Very shortly, because of financial problems it appears the LONG BRANCH EXCURSION HOUSE was almost immediately sold and actually reopened on July 1, 1873 as the EAST END HOTEL!

Since the Long Branch Excursion House apparently existed for only ten days, this advertisement for the new East End Hotel only refers to the former "Arlington House" - there is no mention of the Long Branch Excursion House!

"Excursion House" seems to have remained more of a popular name rather than an official name. It was reported in the *New York Times* in May of 1875 that "The East End House is the excursion house." This is confirmed in another comment in the same newspaper three years later:

> "The East End Hotel is situated at the north end of "the Branch," and besides being an "excursion house" for permanent boarders, it offers a comfortable home at lower rates than any of the larger hotels."[7]

The newly renamed East End Hotel, was described as:

> "... situated at the northern end of the bluff, over a mile from the West End, and only a few rods from the railway station. (By 1878 there was an "Excursion Platform" a block before the depot on the west end of the hotel property which excursionists found to be more convenient.)

> It is an immense structure, accommodating 200 permanent guests, besides affording unrivaled accommodations for excursionists. For permanent boarders, it offers a comfortable home at lower rates than any large hotel in the watering place.

> Messrs. J. B. Smith and Company, took charge of the house towards the close of the last season, and their management has been very successful and satisfactory.

> The grounds belonging to the house are very extensive, and embrace nearly twenty acres. Large and airy dining-rooms, spacious parlors, magnificent piazzas, and a large ball-room are provided, and all these accommodations with excellent bathing facilities, and a good table, are afforded at the reasonable rates of from $2.50 to $3 per day.

> For excursions, the East End offers surpassing inducements in the way of lawns, croquet, and ball-grounds, good beach, and large halls, for all of which no charge whatever is made. Children are delighted with the playgrounds, wherein they may romp and play, and, by their innocent recreation, cultivate ruddy cheeks, glowing health, and a vigorous constitution.

> Parties are at liberty to bring their own provisions in baskets, or to purchase their lunch for very reasonable rates at the well stocked lunch-table provided by the proprietors.

> The following are the rates for excursion parties from New York:

				EACH
50 and less than	100	persons		$ 1.50
100	"	200	"	1.25
200	"	300	"	1.15
300	"	400	"	1.05
400	"	500	"	1.00

> For large parties special rates; children under twelve half fare. Arrangements may be made with the general ticket agent of the New Jersey Southern Railroad, Mr. C. P. McFadden, Long Branch."[8]

A detailed description of the Arlington House has yet to be found. However, the obscure Pach stereograph (ca. 1871) used at the beginning of this chapter has photographically preserved the architecture of this building when it was the Arlington House. It is also possible to identify part of the original Atlantic Hotel in that same stereograph. Another Pach stereograph (ca. 1873) has preserved the East End Hotel. Even though there are obvious structural changes, that image is still readily identifiable as the old Arlington House.

Colonel Jim Fisk and railroad tycoon Jay Gould were involved with the Atlantic Hotel in 1870. That partnership appears to have lasted little more than a year.

By June 30, 1880, Long Branch entrepreneur John Hoey and a few other gentlemen apparently purchased the East End Hotel and "are running it in a first-class manner." A few months later, however, a savage storm washed away part of the bluff in front of the hotel and severely damaged the building. The hotel was closed and torn down the following year.

Eventually, in the late 1890s, the property was acquired by Long Branch resident Nate Salsbury who was an astute investor. Salsbury, famous in his day, was William F. "Buffalo Bill" Cody's business partner and manager of Buffalo Bill's Wild West show. In 1900, Salsbury built nine splendid cottages on the former EAST END HOTEL grounds. He named the houses for native American tribes who were represented in the show, and the entire complex was known as "The Reservation." All but one of the houses were demolished in the 1980s, and the site is now Seven Presidents Ocean-front Park, part of the Monmouth County Park System.

The EAST END HOTEL

PACH STEREOGRAPH #LBU 301, 1873

111

"The arrival of the train at Long Branch Depot."
FRANK LESLIE'S ILLUSTRATED NEWSPAPER, JULY 26, 1873

The Way It Was...

Eager guests flocked to the Long Branch grand hotels during the Victorian years with high hopes that their summer vacations would be perfect. As evidenced in the illustrations and writings of the era, they scurried from trains and steamboats to waiting horse drawn cabs. A visit to a grand hotel was a once in a lifetime visit for some. For others, it was a way of life. Anxious to relax and escape the commotion and the unbearable heat of the crowded cities, they fancied idyllic sunny days and gentle breezes. They usually got what they came for, but nothing is ever totally predictable. The summer sojourners' dreams did not include the realities of storms, humidity, mosquitos, and occasional disorderly people who caused problems for unsuspecting visitors.

The delectable food and fine service at the grand hotels usually proved to be impeccable, but of course there was no doubt a bad meal served now and then. Despite the use of parasols, hats, and homemade lotions, an occasional sunburn probably caused some discomfort. The vacation experience could also be affected by the ups and downs of winning or losing at the racetrack. Nevertheless, the images of elegance and grace overshadow these negative aspects of Victorian life at Long Branch.

"The Great August Storm - Guests of the Ocean Hotel, *Long Branch,
witness the fury of the storm at night. Sketched by D. C. Hitchcock."*
Frank Leslie's Illustrated Newspaper, August 30, 1873

*"Peeping Tom of Long Branch –
The surprise party that waited on an inquisitive
young man from Connecticut."*
The Days Doings, August 10, 1872

One cannot expect hotels built mostly of wood in the early nineteenth century to have survived. If they did, they probably couldn't pass present day health standards or fire safety laws. Because so many old Victorian hotels did burn is the reason why there are such stringent fire codes today. Eventually, all the grand old Long Branch hotels disappeared, either being destroyed by fire or being demolished. There are none left on Ocean Avenue today, and unfortunately some of them have been so long forgotten that no one even seems to know what happened to them. The decline, almost to the point of extinction, of most of the grand hotels at the Jersey Shore is one of the most noticeable changes that occurred in the late nineteenth and early twentieth century.

What was considered an elegant way of life in those bygone days might be frowned upon today as less than acceptable. Obviously there were no televisions, computers, radios or air conditioning in the hotels. The guest's rooms were quite Spartan, the plumbing was rudimentary and the linens utilitarian. Some people today might consider the lack of these improvements a blessing in this hectic world of computer chat rooms and cell phones. Live conversation was the great American pastime. People talked to each other. People talked about each other; people still do but in a variety of ways.

Besides conversation, the hotel guests participated in many activities described in this book including dining, bathing, strolling, driving horses and carriages on Ocean Avenue, playing billiards, croquet, or bowling, listening to band concerts and dancing at hops. Sometimes reading or just sitting and watching the surf was the best activity of all – and many people long to do just that today!

The festivities at the grand hotels did not end at sunset. The bands played on and people danced and talked into the night. From the hotel verandahs and the beaches they observed the beauty of the evening stars and listened to the gentle sounds of the sea.

This 1872 engraving from *APPLETON'S JOURNAL* – a view of a new moon above the glowing lights of the "grand hotels" on Ocean Avenue – tells the story far better than any closing words and truly illustrates the way it was at Long Branch so many years ago.

LONG BRANCH FROM THE SEA AT NIGHT.

Footnotes

The Early Years

1 - *AMERICAN DAILY ADVERTISER*, Dunlap and Claypoole, Phila., May 19, 1792

2 - *THE AMERICAN GAZETTEER*, Jedidiah Morse, Boston, 1797

3 - *THE KNICKERBOCKER, NEW YORK MONTHLY MAGAZINE*, N.Y., September, 1839

4 - *TANNER'S CENTRAL UNITED STATES GUIDEBOOK*, 1841

5 - Letter. Wm. R. Morris from Calif. to Red Bank, N.J. September 11, 1853

6 - *NEW YORK TRIBUNE*, June 19, 1860

7 - *MONMOUTH DEMOCRAT*, July 19, 1860

8 - *NEW YORK TIMES*, August 8, 1865

9 - *EVERY SATURDAY*, August 21, 1871

10 - *FRANK LESLIE'S ILLUSTRATED NEWSPAPER*, 1872

11 - *HARPER'S WEEKLY*, August 23, 1873

12 - *POPULAR RESORTS AND HOW TO REACH THEM*, Bachelder, J.B., Boston, 1875

13 - *SUMMER EXCURSION ROUTES*, Pennsylvania Railroad, 1879

14 - *HARPER'S WEEKLY*, September 1, 1883

15 - *THE NEW JERSEY COAST AND PINES*, Gustav Kobbé, Short Hills, N.J., 1889

The Fashionable Life

1 - *DAILY GRAPHIC*, July 18, 1877

2 - *BRIGHTONS OF AMERICA*, J. H. Schenck, 1878

3 - *THE ILLUSTRATED LONDON NEWS*, September 4, 1875

The Ocean Piers

1 - *NEW YORK TIMES*, May 1875

2 - *SUMMER EXCURSION ROUTES*, Pennsylvania Railroad, Phila., Pa., 1879

3 - *FRANK LESLIE'S ILLUSTRATED NEWSPAPER*, June 1879

4 - *NEW YORK TIMES*, July 1879

5 - *AMERICAN SEASIDE RESORTS*, Taintor Brothers, Pub., N.Y., 1881

6 - *LONG BRANCH RECORD*, Feb. 3, 1893

Hotels

STETSON HOUSE – WEST END HOTEL

1 - *THE LONG BRANCH NEWS*, June 22, 1866

2 - *THE LONG BRANCH NEWS*, June 29, 1866

3 - *THE LONG BRANCH NEWS*, June 19, 1866

4 - *THE LONG BRANCH NEWS*, July 6, 1866

5 - *HARPER'S WEEKLY*, August 14, 1869

6 - *BRIGHTONS OF AMERICA*, J. H. Schenck, 1878

7 - *WHAT TO DO AT LONG BRANCH*, R.F. & C.P. Dearborn, N.Y., 1874

THE HOWLAND HOUSE

1 - *ALBUM OF LONG BRANCH: A SERIES OF PHOTOGRAPHIC VIEWS*. With text, J.H.Schenck, New York, 1868

2 - *WHAT TO DO AT LONG BRANCH*, Dearborn, 1874

3 - *BRIGHTONS OF AMERICA*, J. H. Schenck, 1878

IAUCH'S HOTEL – HOTEL PANNACI

1 - *ENTERTAINING A NATION*, WPA, State of N.J., 1940

2 - *NEW YORK TIMES*, June 26, 1869

3 - *THE LONG BRANCH NEWS*, July, 1869

4 - *THE LONG BRANCH NEWS*, August, 1869

5 - *NEW YORK TIMES*, May, 1877

6 - *Long Branch Daily Record*, June, 1907

THE UNITED STATES HOTEL

1 - *NEW YORK TRIBUNE*, July 29, 1848

2 - *FRANK LESLIE'S ILLUSTRATED NEWSPAPER*, August 22, 1857

3 - *FRANK LESLIE'S ILLUSTRATED NEWSPAPER*, June 19, 1858

4 - *ALBUM OF LONG BRANCH:A SERIES OF PHOTOGRAPHIC VIEWS*, Schenck, 1868

5 - *WHAT TO DO AT LONG BRANCH*, Dearborn, 1874

THE CENTRAL HOTEL

1 - *LONG BRANCH NEWS*, June, 1873

2 - *WHAT TO DO AT LONG BRANCH*, Dearborn, 1874

3 - *WHAT TO DO AT LONG BRANCH*, Dearborn, 1874

The Mansion House

1 - *New York Herald*, August 24, 1861

2 - *Long Branch News*, 1866

3 - *Frank Leslie's Illustrated Newspaper*, July 15, 1865

4 - *What To Do At Long Branch*, Dearborn, 1874

The Continental - Ocean Hotel

1 - *What To Do At Long Branch*, Dearborn, 1874

The Metropolitan Hotel

1 - *New York Times*, August 8, 1865

2 - *New York Times*, August 15, 1865

3 - *Long Branch News*, July 3, 1873

4 - *What To Do At Long Branch*, Dearborn, 1874

5 - *New York Times*, 1875

The Atlantic – Arlington – Long Branch Excursion House – East End Hotel

1 - *Long Branch News*, August 7, 1866

2 - *Long Branch News*, August 1867

3 - *Long Branch News*, August 1867

4 - *Album of Long Branch*, Schenck, 1868

5 - *New York Herald*, June 28, 1869

6 - *Long Branch News*, July 2, 1873

7 - *New York Times*, May 1875

8 - *New York Times*, May 1878

Bibliography

Books and Booklets

Appletons' General Guide to the United States and Canada,
    D.Appleton & Co., Pub., N.Y., 1888

Bachelder, J.B., *Popular Resorts and How to Reach Them*,
    Boston, 1875

Cook, Joel, *Brief Summer Rambles*,
    J. B. Lippincott, Pub., Phila., 1882

Dearborn, R.F. & C.P., *What To Do At Long Branch*, N.Y., 1874

Kobbé, Gustave, *The New Jersey Coast and Pines*, Short Hills, N.J., 1889

Karnoutsos, *New Jersey Women*, New Jersey Historical Commission, Department of State,
    Trenton, NJ, 1997

Lester, Katharine Morris, *Historic Costume*, The Manual Arts Press, Peoria, Illinois, 1925.

Monmouth Park Jockey Club, *From Mauve to Modern*, 1954

Morse, Jedidiah, *The American Gazetteer*, Boston, 1797

Moss Jr., George H., *Another Look at Nauvoo to the Hook*,
    Ploughshare Press, Pub., Sea Bright, N.J., 1990

Moss Jr., George H., *Steamboat to the Shore, A Pictorial History of the Steamboat Era
    in Monmouth County, N.J.*, Ploughshare Press, Pub., Sea Bright, N.J. 1991

Moss, Jr., George H., *Double Exposure Two. Stereographic Views of the Jersey Shore
    (1859 - 1910) and Their Relationship to Pioneer Photography*, Ploughshare Press,
    Pub., Sea Bright, N.J., 1995

"Paul, John, " (Charles H. Webb), *Sea-Weed and What We Seed*,
    Carleton & Co., Pub., N.Y., 1876

Pennsylvania Railroad, *Summer Excursion Routes*, Phila., 1879

Schenck, J.H., *A Complete Descriptive Guide of Long Branch, N.J.*,
    Trow & Smith, Pub., N.Y., 1868

Schenck, J.H., *Album of Long Branch. A Series of Photographic Views*, With text.
    John F. Trow, Pub., N.Y., 1868

Schenck, J.H., *Brightons of America*, 1878

Statia, W.E., *Hotel List and Guide*, Portland, Maine, 1875

Taintor, *American Seaside Resorts*, N.Y., 1881

Tanner, *Central United States Guidebook*, 1841

Ulyat, William C., *Life At The Sea Shore*, Princeton, N.J., 1880

W.P.A., State of N.J, *Entertaining A Nation*, City of Long Branch, N.J., 1940

Newspapers and Magazines

Appleton's Journal

Daily Graphic

Day's Doings

Every Saturday

Frank Leslie's Illustrated Newspaper

Frank Leslie's Popular Monthly

Harper's Bazar

Harper's New Monthly Magazine

Harper's Weekly

Long Branch News

Long Branch Record

Monmouth Democrat

New York Daily Graphic

New York Times

New York Herald

The Knickerbocker - New York Monthly Magazine

*All illustrations in this book, unless otherwise credited,
are from the Moss Archives.*

*Throughout the book contemporary usage, spelling and punctuation
have been retained to preserve the accuracy of the quoted material.*

Book Design and Production
KENNETH E. HOWITT

Printed by
THE RIVERVIEW PRESS
Little Silver, New Jersey